THE QUEEN MOTHER'S FAMILY AND ITS CONNECTIONS WITH THE CROWNS OF SCOTLAND AND ENGLAND

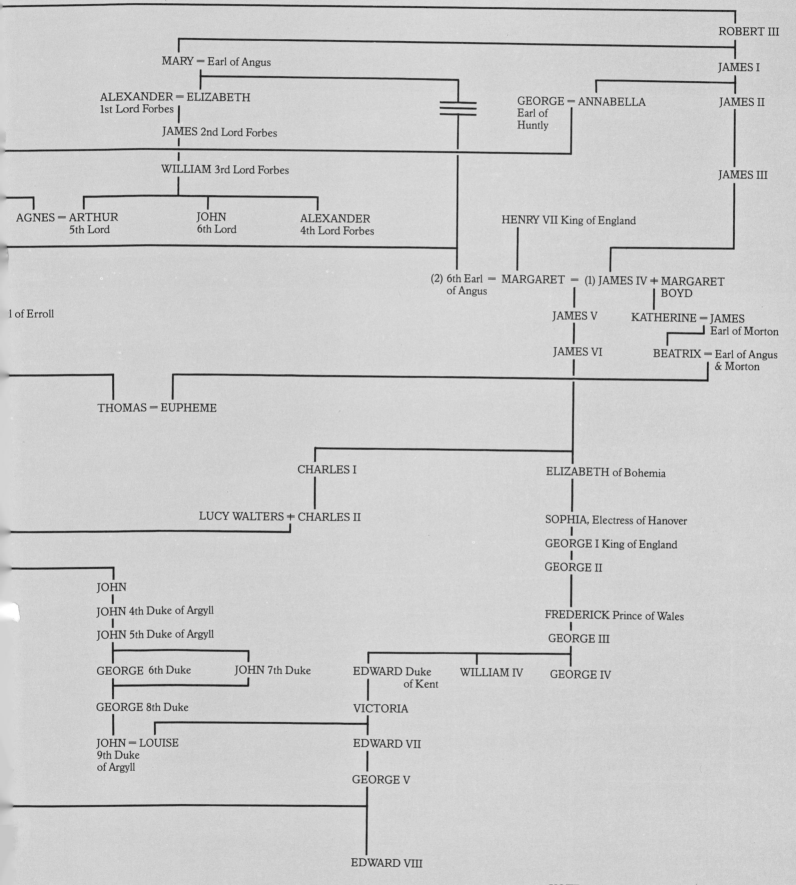

NOTE: + denotes illegitimate union: child born out of wedlock.

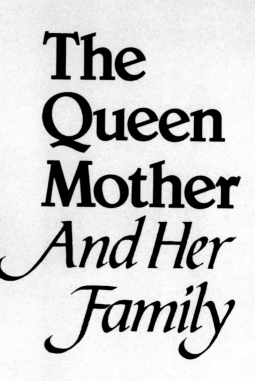

The Queen Mother
And Her Family

The Queen Mother
And Her Family

Trevor Hall

BRITISH HERITAGE PRESS

Foreword by His Grace the Duke of Beaufort, KG, GCVO, former Master of the Horse.

I am pleased to write a few appreciative words about Queen Elizabeth the Queen Mother as a foreword to this large and colourful book devoted to Her Majesty and her family.

I happen to be the same age as Queen Elizabeth – we were both born in 1900 – and I have had the privilege of knowing Her Majesty since 1917, when I was a cadet at the Military College at Sandhurst, and Her Majesty came to stay there with the Earl of Airlie who commanded a company at the College. Since then, I have had the honour of meeting Her Majesty on very many important occasions, and as Master of the Horse I did my best to see to Her Majesty's comfort especially at the last Coronation, but also on the many other occasions when Her Majesty has driven in one of the royal carriages.

This book emphasises Queen Elizabeth's close family life, and as a distant relative by marriage I am pleased once again to be welcoming her here at Badminton for the Cheltenham Races in March. She is also, of course, very well known not only in Britain but in that wider family throughout the old Empire and new Commonwealth which, for so many years, she has loyally and enthusiastically served. I am sure I speak for every reader of this book, for whom the Queen Mother and her daughter the Queen are the two most popular ladies in the country, when I say that we all wish her many more happy years of continuing good health.

Beaufort.

The humble fish-bone has rarely achieved the distinction of becoming remotely notorious, though there are stories enough to link some of the more wretched and unassuming objects of every-day life with phenomenal influences on the course of world history. Cleopatra's asp, Robert the Bruce's spider and Sir Isaac Newton's apple have all been credited with an assured place in the annals of man. Late one Sunday evening in November 1982, these and other historical catalysts were emulated by a fish-bone which lodged in the throat of none other than Queen Elizabeth the Queen Mother during a party at Royal Lodge Windsor where Her Majesty was entertaining a group of family and friends to dinner.
The sight of this gathering of eminent worthies doing their best to slap the offending foreign body from the royal gullet must have been less than dignified, and all concerned will be grateful that the incident took place in private rather than in public.

During their very popular tour of Australia in 1927, the Duke and Duchess of York attended many civic receptions, braving the bad weather to show their appreciation of the welcome, (above) in Brisbane and (left) in Newcastle. On 9th May the Duke opened the new Federal Parliament in Canberra (See Page 4).

The sheer panic which must at times have seized the guests at the thought that their attempts might prove fruitless, and that the life of one of Britain's most august citizens might be in serious danger must have been positively unspeakable.
Ultimately the Queen Mother's physician, Dr John Clayton, was called in and, after consultation with the Queen's physician, Dr John Batten, it was decided to commit the royal victim to hospital and, not for the first time in her life, she was driven up to London to be admitted for an operation. She was accompanied on this occasion by Princess Margaret, her younger daughter and one of her guests that evening, who stayed at the hospital during the course of the operation.

The hospital – King Edward VII's Hospital for Officers, in Marylebone – received its unexpected patient at 1.30 in the morning, and the operation which took place shortly afterwards proved comparatively simple and certainly successful. As on every other occasion when she has attended the hospital in the past, the Queen Mother proved a model patient, and almost scorned the great public concern for her well-being by discharging herself a day earlier than everyone expected. "For a woman of her age," said one of the hospital staff, "her constitution is quite remarkable. After coming round from the anaesthetic, she was bubbling and cheerful for the rest of her stay."
With hindsight the entire episode, though it lasted only two days, seems to have provoked a most disproportionate amount of popular attention – the sort that keeps the ear glued to the radio and the eye casting around for the latest newspaper headline or billboard. The crowds which gathered outside the hospital and the never-ending telephone calls to Clarence House

throughout the period of public knowledge of the crisis may appear to have given the incident an undue degree of significance. Of course, that is a question of priorities, and for a nation beset by one of the biggest post-war depressions and in the grip of almost unprecedented unemployment, the minutiae of a fairly routine, if emergency operation on a Queen Dowager may not rank as being of earth-shattering importance. What the commotion did display, however, was the degree and spontaneity of what King George V rather bashfully acknowledged as the "love" of ordinary people – and the media who exist to feed them their information – for this most rewarding of royal figures, and the feeling that because her weekly appearances in public have of late fallen far behind those of most other members of her family in number, she has been taken rather too much for granted. It was, after all, ironically telling that on the day of her admission to hospital, the results of a poll taken by a reputable firm of researchers into popular opinion was published, in which the Queen Mother herself was rated best at carrying out public duties. Her Majesty's emergence from hospital on 23rd November helped put things right: the full weight of London's press and broadcasting media were on the spot to welcome her, along with some three hundred vociferous well-wishers. For her part, she stood cheerfully on the threshold acknowledging the

The Queen Mother has always been willing to take time out of formal engagements to talk to the people, as during the Australian tour at Gatton (overleaf, top) on 6th April and at Clifton (above) the previous day, when Mr Hendrickson told how he formed part of the guard of honour for Queen Alexandra sixty years earlier. (Left) the Duke and Duchess were presented with a gold nugget at Ballarat and (overleaf, bottom) the Duchess inspected Girl Guides in Melbourne.

public acclaim with her now legendary smile, her customary sheer enjoyment of a little bit of good natured fuss, and above all the time and the will to reward the patience of the photographers with the opportunity to obtain photographs that would please any picture desk editor. It

was even possible to suspect that amid the gratitude for the successful outcome of an incident which could have gone horribly wrong, the Queen Mother was rather enjoying the mischievous twist of fate which had suddenly steered the nation's glance towards her presence.

"All's well that ends well" might well be the family motto for the Queen Mother's long and distinguished line of ancestors. Like most noble families whose histories have been inextricably bound up with national politics and aristocratic machination, hers can boast a pretty rollicking ancestry, though it has borne its share of defeat and disgrace amid its record of success, honour and respect. Willie Hamilton, the Member of Parliament most frequently denounced as the thorn in the side of the monarchy's flesh, has described the Queen Mother's

ancestry as "poorish by aristocratic standards," and whatever this may mean in his own jaundiced and often abusive mind, it is true that her forefathers have until comparatively recently kept themselves very much to themselves in the six hundred years since they first enjoyed the taste of royal favour.

That came when, late in the fourteenth century Sir John Lyon, Queen Elizabeth's ancestor by nineteen generations married Jean, one of two daughters of Robert II, King of Scotland and grandson of the famous Robert the Bruce. Shortly beforehand, Sir John had been granted the thanage of Glamis after several years of royal service, and his marriage brought him additional lands in the form of nearby Tannadyce as well (possibly, for records are by no means precise) as his knighthood. His great-grandson

Patrick became a Peer of the Scottish Parliament and was created the first Lord Glamis in 1445, the date from which the succession of the family's aristocratic titles begins.

There was a desultory but bloody period of intense royal disfavour when King James V conceived that the Glamis family were involved in plotting against him. Both John, seventh Lord Glamis, and his brother George were imprisoned by him while, by sheer coincidence, the widow of the sixth Baron Bowes, an ancestress on the other side of the family, was burnt as a witch in 1537 after having also been accused of designs against the King. Elsewhere in the family, beheadings, deaths while escaping royal custody, and wholesale forfeiture of lands seemed to tumble over one another with monotonous regularity, but with the death of James V and the accession of Mary Queen of Scots, the pressure was lifted and those who survived secured their release from prison and the repossession of property.

Better times were ushered in with the accession of James VI as James I of England in 1603: Patrick, the ninth Lord Glamis, was made a Privy Councillor and given the title of Earl of Kinghorne. Despite some embarrassing family support for the anti-Catholic League of the Covenant in the years that followed, and an even more embarrassing debt of £400,000 which the third Earl inherited and could only liquidate by a life of "frugality and prudence," the family's title was extended within two more generations to include Strathmore, and its members entered into a long period of grace with Britain's monarchy. Real, fluid prosperity, however, did not arrive until the middle of the 18th century, when the ninth Earl married Eleanor Bowes, the only child of a wealthy industrialist from County Durham. His estates covered much of the county, parts of Yorkshire and land in Hertfordshire, and he almost gladly transferred them to the Lyon family on condition that they changed their name to Bowes. This strange *quid pro quo*, the perverse result of greed and snobbery by today's standards, but entirely justifiable in the context of the hard realities of contemporary aristocratic life at the crossroads of the industrial revolution, was agreed to without much demur, though when the old man died, the Earl did a partial *volte-face* and combined both names in the family name of Lyon-Bowes. A century later the 13th Earl, the Queen Mother's grandfather, redressed the balance somewhat by calling himself Bowes-Lyon and there, with a coat of arms quartered by bows and lions to prove it, it has remained ever since.

If, as Willie Hamilton would no doubt insist, that is a poorish direct ancestry, he might concede differently on the question of the Queen Mother's descent through the various female lines. There are, as most people know, a whole range of utterly common names in that part of her lineage – Webb, Tucker, Browne, Grimstead and the like – indeed it is the profusion of these old yeoman names which account for the fact that the royalty element in Queen Elizabeth II's ancestry compares rather badly with that of Prince Philip's. Nevertheless, the Queen Mother's long and exciting Scottish ancestry is matched by lines traced back to Owen Glendower, the Wellesley family, Robert E. Lee and

it was not the case in the Strathmore household eighty years ago.

It was headed by Claude Bowes-Lyon who, as Lord Glamis, was the heir apparent to the Earldom of Strathmore and Kinghorne at the time of Elizabeth's birth. He was a man of simple country tastes – a good shot, a conscientious farmer and a fresh air and exercise fiend. He took his duties as Lord Lieutenant of the county of Angus seriously but without pomposity and he was a devout, plain Christian who deplored social excesses as no doubt he deplored the prospect of an Edwardian age in the grip of moral laxity. His wife – now at nearly 38, a mother for the eighth time – was a first cousin of the 6th Duke of Portland and the prestige of their marriage nearly twenty years before owed as much to her impeccable

The Duke and Duchess of York at Beandesert in April 1927 (below). Among the Australian tour's lighter moments was the presentation by two Red Cross children of a bouquet to the Duchess at Maitland (left).

credentials as to her illustrious kinship. Her mastery of all the recognised Victorian accomplishments, including fine musical tastes and great sympathy with the arts would have done credit to any Jane Austen heroine, and she coupled them with what was then considered to be more adventurous pursuits, such as politics and botany, in which she proved herself equally talented. A stickler for hard work, she drummed its rationale into her children, telling them in a mixture of period moralism and sheer native verve, "Life is for living and working at. If you find anything or anybody a bore, it is your own fault" – right enough, it seems, in those days of unparalleled leisure and privileged opportunity. Her knowledge was extensive; her quest for increasing it insatiable: she was perhaps the Strathmores' equivalent of the then Princess Louis of Battenberg, whom her grandson, the future Prince Philip, Duke of Edinburgh, described as a "walking encyclopaedia." Above all, she was worshipped by all her children for her prodigious

George Washington. And, however much a Member of Parliament might grudgingly admit of the Queen Mother's connections, her husband King George VI had no hesitation in using his in-laws' surname as an *incognito* on one of his most important journeys of the Second World War – his Mediterranean tour of 1943 was undertaken in the name of General Lyon. Ultimately it is worth considering that in contrast to the heavy accent on German descent that in the 18th and 19th centuries became the hallmark of the British Royal Family, the Queen Mother has provided her daughter's lineage with British names to the extent of almost 50% in an ancestry otherwise crammed with representatives from all the Protestant and many of the Catholic and Orthodox houses of Europe.

In deference to the now failing tradition that a lady's age is not the subject of public discussion, references to the Queen Mother's age have frequently avoided the personal truth. Precision has, however, been conveniently maintained by virtue of the fact that, as we are always being told, she is "as old as the century." It sounds like an achievement, and as time goes on that is precisely what it is becoming. The most eminent of those who can boast a connection with the age of Queen Victoria, the Hon. Elizabeth Bowes-Lyon was born on Saturday, 4th August 1900. The inevitable stereotype of life among the aristocracy at the turn of the century would lead us to imagine that she was born into a world of social splendour, domestic discipline and moral austerity, but while it was so for the family of her future husband,

wisdom and her concern for their welfare and the confident, gentle and secure manner in which she brought them up. Much is made of Queen Elizabeth's Scottish ancestry but it is pedantically a falsehood to say that she is a Scottish Queen. She was born no more than thirty miles from London in a house at St Paul's Walden Bury, near Hatfield in Hertfordshire. Built by Sir William Chambers in the mid-eighteenth century it was and is a small mansion of warm red brick, set on rising ground, even now enjoying the tranquillity – rare in an area shot through with motorways – afforded by massive, ancient trees, thick woods and vast expanses of lawn, where the battle to keep the daisies down has long since been conceded. It was the weekend retreat of the then Lord and Lady Glamis from their London House, 20 St James's Square where, since they took it on lease in 1906, they lived for most of the year. But for three or four months, after the London season ended, the family moved up to Scotland to spend the late summer and autumn at Glamis Castle, "heavy with atmosphere" as one of its guests described it in 1922,

"sinister, lugubrious . . .", redolent with the macabre legends of Macbeth, Duncan and Malcolm II.

There was nothing lugubrious about family life for Lady Elizabeth, as she became in 1904 when her father became the 14th Earl of Strathmore and Kinghorne. By then her mother had produced yet another child – the last of nine – a boy called David, born in 1902. The friendship formed between these "two Benjamins" as their mother called them, shaped and fulfilled their joint childhood, endured for almost sixty years and became famous for its intensity and sincerity. He became the companion who made her presence among so many older siblings palatable – she became an aunt at the age of ten, and one of her older brothers died when she was only eleven. It was with David that Lady Elizabeth sat through lessons – drawing, painting, music and dancing – which their mother personally supervised. When, as was the social fashion, David was sent away to Eton in 1912, she felt so deserted that she too was allowed to go to boarding school. But the experiment failed and, after a

term's abject unhappiness, she was back in the family schoolroom, yearning for the holidays when the friendship would be resumed with renewed vigour. Together they romped through nurseries with their

huge rocking horses, ran through the lush, green, hedge-lined avenues at St Paul's or played hide and seek in the narrow-windowed attics at Glamis. Together they read books, looked after a variety of pets, or dressed up in historical costumes from a massive chest – all under the eye of the Strathmores' tried and trusted governess Mrs Clara Cooper Knight. "Allah," as she was known to her charges, was dependable enough to have been indispensable to the family for almost twenty years. Indeed after the children had grown up, one of them, Lady Elphinstone, employed her to look after her own children, and in 1926 Lady Elizabeth herself, then Duchess of York, brought her into royal service to supervise Princess Elizabeth. It was a tribute to the high regard in which she was held after seventeen years as governess to the young princesses that her funeral in 1946 was attended by Queen Elizabeth herself, who commented: "She mothered us all."

Time invariably invests a half-forgotten age with the golden tinge of vague nostalgia, and an Edwardian childhood in the immutable world of the aristocracy before the lamps went out is as liable to this

As a pupil she was questioning and adept, if a little mischievous; she enjoyed the housewifely virtues of sewing and shopping, and showed an early liking, if not exactly an expertise, for horse-riding – a pastime which was not to last beyond adolescence. Escapades, whether permitted or illicit, were both frequent and imaginative. She and David would relive Scottish battles of the past along the ramparts of Glamis Castle, tipping cold water from its many vantage points onto unsuspecting members of the family, or even visitors, below. Or they would set up dens in the attics of the brew-house at St Paul's, using a ladder which was so rotten that no adults sent in search of them would dare use it. Indeed, during her early twenties, in a brief literary passion (which her senior grandson seems to have followed with *The Old Man of Lochnagar*, Lady Elizabeth wrote a story for children set in surroundings which, as in most first novels, smacked of the autobiographical. It described a wood at the bottom of a garden, statues covered in moss, the solemn burial of dead birds and a "flea house" where a little girl and her brother "go and hide from their Nurse." There was no disclaimer that any similarities to life at St Paul's Walden Bury were purely coincidental!

As a teenager she used to spend the winters with each of her two grandmothers who lived on the French and Italian Rivieras. These holidays gave her the opportunity to supplement her French conversation, learned from whom her brother called "a succession of French gover-nesses," to the degree of fluency which has characterised her delivery ever since. She also developed a precocious talent for gardening, turning her meagre 6 x 12 feet plot at Glamis into a triumph of colour with a succession of polyanthus, roses and grape-hyacinth. David shared her enjoyment of the outdoor world – he himself was to become an authority on trees and shrubs, gardening and land-scaping – and it was with him that Lady Elizabeth, walking among Scotland's moorland heathers or fishing in her lakes and rivers, spent the long, late summers of a dying era.

After the worries of the Abdication crisis, the Coronation of King George VI and Queen Elizabeth was an event for public rejoicing. Thousands of people turned out along the route to cheer, (opposite above and opposite below) at Buckingham Palace, which contrasted with the solemnity of the ceremony itself (above and right).

indulgence as any. Queen Elizabeth herself, in a 1948 broadcast, referred to her upbringing as "my own happy childhood," and there is indeed a general consensus that no place, event or personality of those early years clouded the infant mind. Lady Elizabeth was, according to her nurse, "an exceptionally happy, easy baby, crawling early, running at thirteen months and speaking very young;" and she was soon the adored, and perhaps a little indulged, baby of a family whose way of life was bright, playful and loving. She learned Bible story after Bible story at her mother's knee, showed a penchant for flowers, and a love of parties and children's games.

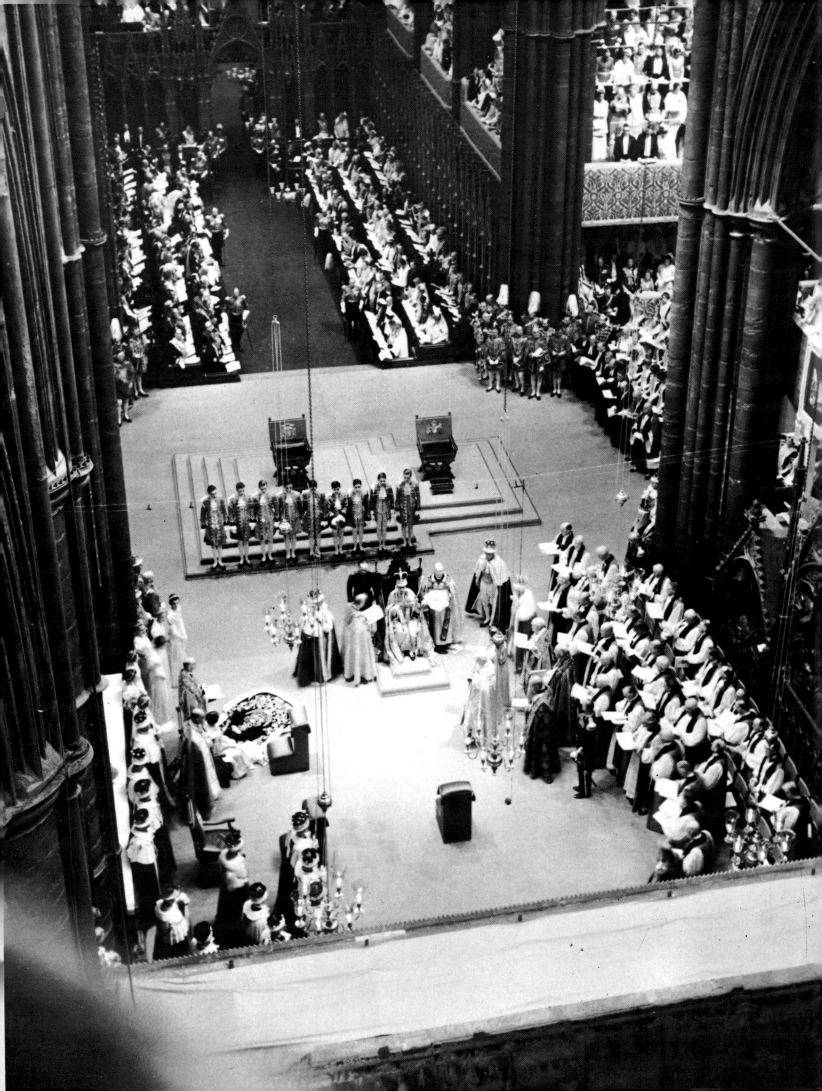

The scene in Westminster Abbey soon after the moment of coronation (opposite), with the new King seated on the throne of St Edward. (Above and right) the Royal Family appears on the balcony of Buckingham Palace after the ceremony.

She could not fail to remember the day which signified its end. It was August 4th 1914, a Bank holiday and, more to the point, her fourteenth birthday, and she celebrated it with a visit to London's Coliseum Theatre where the family had rented a box. At some time during the long variety performance which she had gone to watch the news broke, perhaps unofficially, to end the month-old speculation on the likelihood of war, and the theatre buzzed with rumours. At the end of the show she emerged into streets she described as "filled with people shouting and full of enthusiasm," as Londoners, fervently patriotic and tragically unsuspecting of its consequences, hailed the beginning of the European conflict with prolonged and rousing cheers. As she lay in bed that night Lady Elizabeth could hear the swell of voices as the entire capital, it seemed, flocked up the Mall to Buckingham Palace to acclaim the man who, less than nine years later, would be her father-in-law.

By the end of that week Lady Elizabeth was travelling north to begin "those awful four years that followed" at Glamis, but even here, up to eight hundred miles from the theatre of war she was not immune from its effects. Within three months of the Declaration, part of Glamis Castle became a convalescent hospital for wounded soldiers, the dining room was converted into a sixteen-bed ward run by Lady Strathmore's third daughter, Rose, who was undergoing training as a nurse. Lady Strathmore herself was there to supervise and, even at the tender age of fourteen, Lady Elizabeth was a willing recruit as, in December 1914 the first of fifteen hundred casualties arrived in khaki uniforms or in the dull blue garb of the hospitals from which they were being transferred. Without qualifications save those of charm, sympathy and helpfulness, she warmed to the possibilities of this unexpected turn of events: she

The unchanging face of monarchy. King George VI (opposite) was crowned seated on St Edward's throne over the Stone of Destiny, as was his daughter, Queen Elizabeth II, 26 years later (above and above right).

took her meals with the wounded visitors, helped them to write letters home, did their shopping for them, played cards and billiards with them, distributed their mail and even brought small presents for them – in short, she played the junior hostess. In addition there were other activities in support of the War effort – public ones, like the manning of stalls during sales of work, and private ones including, like Sister Susie of the tongue-twisting song, sewing shirts for soldiers.

That serene and abiding vision of Lady Elizabeth in wartime is enlivened by the incident of the great fire in which, much to her astonishment, she found herself playing a major part. One day in September 1916 she was the only one of the family to be in the Castle – Rose had already

married, her father and brother had gone out shooting and the convalescent soldiers had been taken to the cinema for the afternoon. In the course of a couple of hours that were later to be described as heroic she had raised the alarm, telephoned three fire brigades, marshalled and detailed jobs to the servants, established a chain of bucket handlers, and organised the beginnings of a salvage operation to save many family heirlooms and treasures from being destroyed. In spite of her efforts the damage was extensive and severe both to the Castle and to its contents, but the local newspaper next morning paid tribute to her part in preventing the worst and she was evidently much amused to find her actions so universally admired.

The event was one of few excitements of those interminable war years and, indeed, desperate did they become even for the privileged families of Britain's aristocracy. The Strathmore clan suffered no less than any other in terms of personal loss: one of Lady

Elizabeth's brothers, Fergus, was killed at the Battle of Loos in September 1915, only days after returning to the front from a short leave to see his only child. Two more brothers – Patrick and "Jock" – were wounded while another brother, Michael, was taken prisoner and was not returned until 1919. In addition, three of Lady Elizabeth's first cousins were killed, an uncle and two more first cousins came home wounded. It was a strenuous tally of death, mutilation and distress, and one which left the once bubbling Lady Strathmore, not yet sixty years of age, debilitated with worry and sorrow.

Youth, however, was on the side of Lady Elizabeth for whom 1919 was the year of her liberation. The London Season habit was not slow in returning after the cessation of hostilities, even though the uncertain and self-conscious resumption of everyday life muted the brilliance of the palmier pre-War days, and the youngest of the Strathmore girls now took full advantage. She returned to

London for the great occasions, such as Royal Ascot and, in July, the national Victory March, and for the more relaxed social enjoyments like parties, receptions and society weddings. It was the year of her social *début,* her "coming-out," and like all *débutantes* of high birth, she was presented to the King and Queen at Court. There followed a succession of invitations to dances, where she immediately won a string of admirers and was generally agreed to be the most accompanied dancer in London. During the next two years she broadened her horizons considerably, visiting several country houses and again playing hostess at Glamis where long weekend house parties included shooting and salmon-fishing expeditions. In 1922, making her first independent journey to France, she accompanied her close friend Diamond Hardinge to Paris, where she made so many friends that, even sixty and more years later, her private visits across the Channel continue. By that time she was widely credited with

drawn in a coach-and-four and quartered in the best house in the land." And one rainy afternoon in 1922 Chips Channon, who was staying at Glamis for a week-end, entertained the other guests, who included the Duke of York, by pretending to foretell Lady Elizabeth's future from the playing cards. Rightly guessing the Duke's feelings for her he predicted "a great and glamorous royal future." She laughed, Channon recorded, "for it was obvious that the Duke of York was much in love with her." And as Queen she several times reminded him of the incident.

It would be trite and ingenuous to ascribe prophetic attributes to any of these stories, particularly as the contacts between the Bowes-Lyons and the Royal

every social grace, from good conversation to a wide range of interests, from tennis and motoring to the domestic accomplishments. Above all she was mature and responsible – one of the soldiers she had looked after during the war had already testified to that as early as 1916: "For her fifteen years she was very womanly, kind-hearted and most sympathetic." Now she was hailed as "the best type of girlhood with a healthy taste for outdoor life . . . (She) is not only a good sportsman but . . clever with her needle and a lover of the arts that go to the making of a happy home." That estimate of her vied for a hearing with a torrent of encomiums which accompanied the news of her engagement in January 1923 to the Duke of York. Except to those in the know, the news was a complete surprise if for no other reason that neither party was publicly known to have been in serious search of a partner. The fate of previous suitors (if any) of Lady Elizabeth is not known, though she inspired the hopes of many. One such was a young American, later Sir Henry Channon who, as "Chips" Channon, became very much part of London Society between the Wars: in 1937, as he watched Queen Elizabeth being crowned consort he "thought of the old days when I called her Elizabeth and was even a little in love with

Following the precedent set by Queen Mary, Queen Elizabeth the Queen Mother attended the Coronation of her daughter Queen Elizabeth II. The Coronation was a blend of old and new; all the traditions were observed, but at the same time television cameras were allowed within the Abbey to record the ceremony.

her." The royal match raised even more eyebrows because it was the reticent, rather dutiful Duke of York who was involved and not his far more dashing, colourful, globetrotting elder brother the Prince of Wales. Stories of varying degrees of credibility have grown up as pointers to the inevitability of Lady Elizabeth's undoubted good fortune. It is said that, as a child, she performed a stately dance with her brother as a party piece, and called herself "Princess Elizabeth." Another tale relates how she was told by a gypsy in a sideshow tent at a Glamis Castle garden party in August 1910 that one day she would become a Queen: she didn't seem to relish the idea even then. In 1917, at the end of his convalescence at Glamis, a soldier signed her autograph book, wishing that its owner "may be hung drawn and quartered – hung in diamonds,

Family were less than tenuous. Lord Strathmore himself conceived an early suspicion of the reliability of a Court which, in the late 19th and early 20th century, permitted and even encouraged a degree of moral turpitude in many of its principal members and the constant vulgarities and excesses of its numerous parasites. It was an attitude which the soundness and dedication of King George V and of the upright Queen Mary had only just begun to change, and the change coincided with Lady Elizabeth's close acquaintance, through their common interest in the Girl Guide movement, with the King's only daughter Princess Mary. By coincidence, the Duke of York had formed friendships with some of Lady Elizabeth's brothers, whose free and easy way of life he envied, and in that capacity was a frequent guest both at Glamis and at St Paul's Walden Bury. But his first conscious meeting with Lady Elizabeth – apart from the legendary encounter at a children's party in 1905 when she picked the cherries off her cakes and gave them to him – came in May 1920. Still known as Prince Albert then – it was a fortnight before his father made him Duke of York in that year's Birthday Honours – he was attending a dance at the London home of Lady Farquhar, and Lady Elizabeth made an impression on him which drove him to court her persistently, and to the exclusion of any other, for the next two and a half years. Another visit to Glamis followed that autumn and again in the autumn of 1921 when, according to the Duke, "Elizabeth is very kind to me. The more I see of her the more I like her." Fortunately for both of them, there were no newspaper reporters or photographers to monitor his progress and turn the whole episode into a soap opera, but the social grapevine fairly hummed with activity and the King and Queen received gratifying reports about their prospective daughter-in-law. Well briefed by Princess Mary and by Lady Airlie, the Queen's close confidante and a neighbour of the Strathmores, King George blessed his son's efforts on his first attempts to

win her hand. "You'll be a lucky fellow if she accepts you," he wrote.

But the proposal was turned down. Innermost thoughts have remained private, and the reasons for Lady Elizabeth's refusal can only be intelligently speculated upon. The most plausible of them hinge upon the almost frightening leap from the easy and relatively quiet world of the landed nobility to the intransigent formality of Court life and an existence in the fierce glare of constant and sometimes highly undesirable publicity. It may have had something to do with her father's earlier, though now less justifiable, distaste for Court life, or to her own apprehension that she might neither make a good wife to a Royal Duke nor be equal to the responsibilities inescapable for anyone who became a member of his family by blood or by marriage. Lady Strathmore put it down to her being "torn between her longing to make Bertie happy and her reluctance to take on the big responsibility which this marriage must bring." In a letter

penned with great sincerity to Lady Airlie, she added, "I do hope he will find a nice wife who will make him happy. I like him so much and," she concluded

with her usual, almost prophetic, perception, "he is a man who will be made or marred by his wife."

Decent form dictated that, for the time being at least, that should be the end of the matter, and the Duke of York was not the sort to ignore the done thing. Being normally frustrated by setbacks, however, and unable respectably to attempt to redress his disadvantage, it is surprising that he took up his cause once again within what seems to have been a relatively short space of time. Late in 1921 the Duke, this time accompanied by his sister, paid another social visit to Glamis for one of the customary end-of-year gatherings and the following February the roles were, if anything, reversed when Lady Elizabeth came to London as one of Princess Mary's bridesmaids for her marriage to Viscount Lascelles. At the wedding breakfast at Buckingham Palace, who should the Duke of York find himself placed next to but Lady Elizabeth!

It seems that later that year, and probably as a result of the frequent references that the Duke made to Lady Elizabeth in his letters to his mother, Queen Mary and her newly-married daughter paid their respects to the Strathmores at Glamis, and

towards the end of 1922 the Duke was there again, preparing the way for his next attempt at winning the lady he had wooed for two years. Early in the New Year the Strathmores came down to London and on the weekend of 12th and 13th January invited the Duke to stay at St Paul's Walden Bury. Both families knew what to expect from this visit and before leaving for Hertfordshire the Duke told his parents that he would telegraph a message to them at Sandringham as soon as he had news for them. On Sunday 13th, the Duke and Lady Elizabeth excused themselves from church – a request that seems to have been granted without the need for explanation – and went for a walk together in the woods which had once been the lady's childhood hideaway. Here the Duke made his second, and successful, proposal of marriage

and soon afterwards a telegram announcing simply "Alright, Bertie" was flashed to the Norfolk countryside, to add a rare touch of magic to the repetitive royal way of life hallowed as immutable for a Sandringham January. "We are delighted and he looks beaming!" Queen Mary enthused in her diary when, on 15th January, the Duke travelled to Sandringham to confirm his good news in person and to obtain his parents' approval. There was no mistaking his elation at the success of his enterprise and the vindication of his determined persistence. He himself admitted "I am very happy and I can only hope that Elizabeth feels the same as I do. I know I am very lucky to have won her over at last." Even the King, habitually strict with his sons and faintly suspicious of their activities and attitudes, was

For a short time during the Coronation ceremony the young Prince Charles was allowed to join his grandmother, and he kept her busy with endless questions (above and facing page, top). A tradition which has become obligatory is that the Royal Family appears on the balcony and the 1953 Coronation was no exception. The Royal Family turned out in force (facing page, below) to wave to the thousands of cheering well-wishers who thronged the roads and pavements outside the Palace.

sufficiently moved to allow this moment of family rejoicing to mark the beginning of a slow but perceptible relaxation, at least in his relations with the Duke of York. His delighted reaction shone through his otherwise rather unimaginative and paternalistic letter of

congratulation after their marriage: "You are indeed a lucky man to have such a charming and delightful wife as Elizabeth. I trust that you both will have many years of happiness before you and that you will be as happy as Mama and I am after you have been married thirty years. I can't wish you more."

By contrast to what has often been suspected in subsequent royal romances, no delay was allowed between the granting of parental consents and the public announcement of the *fait accompli.* The Court Circular recorded the royal engagement with its one customary, heavily-formulated sentence on 16th January and the evening papers and the following day's nationals brimmed with the triumph and congratulation of it all. Headlines ran across full pages, torrents of sub-heads summarising incidental details cascaded down double columns, historians came forth to contribute articles on Lady Elizabeth's ancestry and biography, gossip writers on the ladies' pages fairly weakened at the knees. For a day at least, Mayfair society was indistinguishable from any other community in the country in the intensity of interest over the forthcoming marriage, and Lady Elizabeth was mildly taken aback by it. "We hoped we were going to get a few days' peace," she wrote to a friend. "But the cat is now completely out of the bag and there is no possibility of stuffing him back. I feel very happy but quite dazed." Indeed, no-one seemed other than happy, if a little dazed. The Earl and Countess of Strathmore came to Sandringham with their daughter the following weekend where they saw the King, Queen and the 78-year-old Queen Alexandra as well as the Duke of York. His parents were delighted with the prospective daughter-in-law: the King found her "pretty and charming," the Queen additionally thought she was "so . . . engaging and natural." Both testified to their son's supreme happiness. Everyone, it seemed, was happy. As if by universal consent to the unwritten code which dictates that the more hopeless the human condition the more readily must any opportunity for

and the breezy post-War era which cared little for any reservations Queen Victoria might have had, welcomed its rebirth without hesitation. As Freda Dudley-Ward said (rather grudgingly in the context of the Duke of Windsor's marriage), "Nothing below a Princess was considered suitable for a Prince to marry until Elizabeth Bowes-Lyon came along." But Princess Patricia, the younger daughter of the Duke of Connaught, had married a commoner, Commander Alexander Ramsay, only four years before; Princess Mary herself had already followed suit. There was something vaguely liberating about the King's second son choosing a partner not only from amongst his own compatriots but also palpably for love. It was this element above all else which illustrated the new essence of the monarchical concept after the Great War.

Lady Elizabeth's engagement, marked by the Duke's gift to her of a platinum ring bearing a large Kashmir sapphire and two diamonds, and of a diamond naval-cap badge, was comparatively short. The Press had, rightly as it turned out,

speculated for the end of April, but for some time the prospect of one of King George's rare visits abroad – to Italy – made it impossible to commit him to a date for his son's wedding. The eventual choice of Thursday 26th April left less than three months for preparations to be finalised. It was to be an occasion of considerable splendour, though the King had his own ideas about preserving the dignity of Westminster Abbey, where the ceremony was to be held, and proscribed any untoward profusion of flowers about its sanctified walls and pillars. The choice of Westminster Abbey followed recent precedent – Princess Patricia had been the only one of Queen Victoria's numerous children and grandchildren to be married there, and the Duke of York had the distinction, for the historically minded, of being the first male member of the Royal Family to marry there since Richard II married Anne of Bohemia in 1382 – and the first son of a reigning monarch to do so for over 650 years. Much to widespread disappointment, the new and exciting medium of broadcasting was not to be

diversion be seized, the whole nation, still in the grip of economic recession following a temporary and artificial post-War boom, looked forward eagerly to the coming theatre of royal romance.

No family rose to such instant public attention as the Strathmores, with their long and interesting history, their more recent social connections and the cosy tales of their enviable private lives. Many of the delightful childhood stories which have for sixty years clung to our present Queen Mother took root then, as people who had known her – or claimed to have done – sent their anecdotes and private reminiscences into public circulation. Above all she was taken into the public embrace for what she was – or at least what she seemed to be: personable, attractive, well-dressed, cultured, slightly vulnerable, essentially different, a breath of fresh air. The concept of the royal prince marrying a commoner had survived the ruins of the royal romances of Georgian times,

embraced in the plans for the Abbey ceremony. National broadcasting was then only a year old and what we now take for granted as the great benefit of communication to everyone almost entirely regardless of personal circumstance was viewed in this instance with some distaste. Even as late as 1934, when transmission of the Duke of Kent's marriage to Princess Marina of Greece was being mooted, the Dean and Chapter of Westminster unwittingly bequeathed one of the finest expressions of the dilemmas inherent in reconciling the traditions of the past with an age of almost breathless modernity, refusing the BBC's request to transmit on the grounds that the broadcast might be received by disrespectful people "sitting in Public Houses with their hats on." In 1923 the issue was presumably even more clear-cut and the innovation was not given much of a chance.

By contrast the time-honoured rituals were being played out. On 12th February a special meeting of the Privy Council was called to give formal consent, under the Royal Marriages Act of 1772, to the Duke of York's wedding, and a clerk then spent three days and

almost two dozen quill pens setting out, in illuminated manuscript on parchment, the terms of the Marriage Licence. McVitie & Price of Edinburgh were commissioned to bake the wedding cake, and plans went ahead for London to be decked out as never before, with heavy bunting strung across roads, entwined A's and E's everywhere and three miles of illuminations through the streets of the West End. In a gesture which was to be repeated at subsequent royal weddings, special facilities for incapacitated ex-servicemen to witness the processions at Buckingham Palace were

Distant images of a happy Edwardian childhood. One of the Queen Mother's earliest portraits – the toddler in the highchair (above right) was taken at St Paul's Walden Bury, her parents' Hertfordshire mansion, in 1902. Over sixty years later Maurice Chevalier sang to her "You must have been a beautiful baby," and the smile on her face in the photograph (opposite page) taken at Glamis Castle, the ancestral home in Scotland, when she was seven, has melted many hearts since. Her predilection for pearls – an indispensable part of her adult wardrobe – and for the flowers which have been almost synonymous with her, had obviously already taken hold. As a child, outdoor life was at least as important to her as indoor work and leisure, and the photographs (above and right) taken in about 1906 identify her with life in the country. This element of her being is reflected in the beautiful gardens which she has made her own at Royal Lodge Windsor and the Castle of Mey in north-east Scotland.

arranged – a tactful and considerate concession by a family who knew its debt to millions of war dead and wounded. Less publicised preparations – the design and manufacture of the bride's wedding dress and trousseau – were accompanied by advice and speculation in the papers and magazines of the day as to their final outcome. *Punch* modified its habitual deference with a touch of respectable humour: it quoted an American newspaper which had erroneously referred to the bridegroom as the Duke of New York, and concluded that the mistake was understandable since after all the Duke was "about to enter the united state." The passing of Easter and the promise of Spring intensified the anticipation of Lady Elizabeth's wedding and huge crowds were expected to turn out onto the processional route. A Mrs Sykes of Walthamstow was the first person known to have taken up her position, shortly after midnight on 26th April: she was something of a character, having performed a similar ritual for Princess Mary's wedding fourteen months earlier. By two o'clock a few small gatherings had formed; four hours later the routes were lined, and hawkers of white heather, capitalising out of the bride's Scottish origins, began to do a roaring trade. Seats began to be taken in the Abbey at 9.30 and by ten o'clock, with an hour and a half to go, several parts of the route were seven-deep with people and there were six thousand people outside No. 17 Bruton Street, the unpretentious

Victorian house which had been Lord and Lady Strathmore's London home since 1919 and from which the bride would leave for her wedding.

The Queen Mother has not always been noted for her punctiliousness but on this occasion, with a punctuality which would have done credit to Queen Mary, she emerged from the doorway of No. 17 on the arm of her father and made her way through the cheers and good wishes of the crowd to a waiting carriage. From that moment as she rode unsaluted, and escorted only by mounted policemen – she was still only a commoner – she became what the *Sunday Pictorial* called "the

bridal idol," and the vision of her as she left the carriage and disappeared into the vast Abbey with its awning and red carpet, called forth the most poetic of descriptions. Her wedding dress, designed by Handley-Seymour, affected the fashionable medieval look, draped rather than fitted, ivory rather than pure white. The chiffon moiré gown was panelled across the bodice with horizontal bands of silver lamé ornamented in seed-pearl embroidery, and from waist to hem by a wide vertical band of silver and pearls threaded with ribbon. The short train that fell from her waist was made of tulle over lamé with Nottingham lace – a gesture against the import of foreign lace which at that time was contributing to swingeing unemployment in the Nottingham lace-making industry – and the tulle veil which floated over her otherwise unadorned head was edged with a length of rare Point de Flandres lace lent by Queen Mary, and secured by a chaplet of leaves. Lady Elizabeth's arms were virtually bare, covered by only the shortest of sleeves, and light satin shoes peeped from beneath the hem of the skirt. In her hands she held a bouquet of white roses, the symbol of the House of York, white heather and a sprig of myrtle taken, as

The wedding that launched Lady Elizabeth Bowes-Lyon into over sixty years of the unremitting publicity that comes of being a member of the Royal Family was celebrated on 26th April 1923. Lady Elizabeth, who woke up that morning for the last time as a commoner, left her parents' London home, 17 Bruton Street in Mayfair (left) for Westminster Abbey, where her marriage to the 27-year-old Duke of York was solemnised. Afterwards, Buckingham Palace was the scene of a series of official wedding photographs of the happy couple (opposite, top). The bride chose eight attendants: in the photograph above they are (left to right) her friend, the Hon. Diamond Hardinge, Lady Mary Cambridge – a niece of Queen Mary and now the Duchess of Beaufort, the Hon. Elizabeth Elphinstone – a niece of the bride, Lady Mary Thynne, Lady Katharine Hamilton, the Hon. Cecilia Bowes-Lyon – another of the bride's neices, Lady May Cambridge – only daughter of Princess Alice Countess of Athlone, also niece of Queen Mary, and Miss Betty Cator. The official photograph (right) of the Duke and Duchess of York was taken in 1926.

It was three years before the Duke and Duchess of York became parents, and the birth of their first child in April 1926 thrilled the whole country almost as much as it delighted the baby's immediate family. The birth, christening, indeed the entire childhood of Princess Elizabeth became the focus for a degree of popular interest that has hardly waned in almost sixty years. To an extent, that public curiosity was satisfied by the frequent release of photographs of the growing family, and no photographer caught the close relationship between parents and children more effectively than Marcus Adams. The photograph (below) shows the Duke and Duchess of York with Princess Elizabeth in December 1926, while the affection which has always existed between mother and daughter is beautifully illustrated in his portrait (left) taken in about 1928. This photograph, as well as his 1931 study (opposite page) of the Duke and Duchess with Princess Elizabeth and the year-old Princess Margaret, is reproduced by gracious permission of Her Majesty the Queen.

royal tradition dictated, from a bush at Osborne House which Queen Victoria grew from a similar sprig in her own wedding bouquet. And as, to the sound of Elgar's Bridal March, Lady Elizabeth began her journey up the aisle, she stopped to place her flowers on the tomb of the Unknown Warrior: the myrtle, which was later removed and preserved, became the parent of two fine bushes now flourishing at Royal Lodge, the Queen Mother's Windsor home for over half a century.

It must have been an awesome sight for the bride as she neared her future husband, smartly uniformed as a Group-Captain in the RAF, complete with the resplendent Orders of the Garter and Thistle, the Garter Sash, lanyards and a string of medals. The whole eminence of the Royal Family awaited – the King resplendent in his scarlet Field-Marshal's uniform, the Queen in

silver, the gaunt Queen Alexandra cloaked in ermine, a host of young and elderly princes and princesses, representatives of those branches of Queen Victoria's family who occupied royal establishments in Scandinavia, the Low Countries and the Balkans, and five Indian Princes. The Duke of York, with his groomsman the Prince of Wales in Welsh Guard's uniform, gave his bride the merest, almost furtive, glimpse and the briefest smile as she arrived and, ensconced in solemnity, they scarcely looked at each other during the ceremony. Behind her stood eight bridesmaids in green and white, with white flowers in their hair, and beyond them the congregation of almost three thousand. Before her

stood the Archbishop of Canterbury, Randall Davidson, who solemnised the marriage, conducting the service which included a slight amendment to the Form prescribed by the 1662 Prayer Book, without, of course, calling into question the bride's vow to obey. The ring of yellow gold was fashioned from a nugget mined at Barmouth in mid-Wales for the purpose; the remainder of the nugget was used for the wedding rings of the bride's daughters in 1947 and 1960, her granddaughter Princess Anne in 1973 and ultimately for Diana Princess of Wales in 1981. The address was given by the then Archbishop of York, Cosmo Lang, who was to play a more dramatic role in Lady Elizabeth's life thirteen years later. Almost ominously he

warned her that "You cannot resolve that your wedded life shall be happy, but you can and will resolve that it shall be noble . . . The warm and generous heart of the people takes you today to itself," he continued. "Will you not in response take that heart, with all its joys and sorrows, into your own?" The register awaited the cluster of royal signatures usual on the

rare occasions of this magnitude; "Elizabeth Bowes-Lyon" was modestly entered for the last time beneath the solid, plain signature of "Albert." Over a dozen British and European royalties signed, and witnesses, from the Dowager Empress of All the Russias to the Marquess of Cambridge, together with seven members of the Bowes-Lyon family, several clerics and

(Above left and opposite page) two portrait studies of the 25-year-old Duchess of York with Princess Elizabeth in 1926. Four years later, a second daughter was born, at Glamis Castle: (above) Princess Margaret Rose with her mother in September 1930. All three photographs on these pages were taken by Speaight Ltd and are reproduced by gracious permission of Her Majesty the Queen.

the Prime Minister, Mr Bonar-Law, added their testimony. The day's weather had been far from ideal and the crowds who had gathered for so many hours bore the brunt of some fierce and prolonged April showers. At some point during the morning's proceedings the rain stopped and the sun appeared, satisfying the widespread hope and belief that the bride would be blessed for ever by this overt sign of divine favour. There are, however, conflicting accounts of the transformation: some observers said that the sun came out as the bride entered the Abbey, others that she returned to Buckingham Palace in a "flood of sunlight." Yet another, more romantic, interpretation was placed upon one reporter's staunch conviction that the sun first came streaming through the Abbey windows just as Archbishop Lang's address came to its conclusion, with the words "Good luck in the name of the Lord." The King, whose memory always seemed to be faultless and who noted events with much detail, wrote in his diary that "it stopped raining at 9.30 and the sun actually came out as the Bride entered the Abbey."

There seems little doubt that bright weather awaited the bride and groom as, stopping in their triumphal procession only to bow and curtesy to the King and Queen, they emerged from the Abbey to an enormous barrage of cheering while the powerful strains of Mendelssohn's much-favoured *Wedding March* thundered behind them. The enthusiasm recalled London on Victory Night and the Daily Mirror recorded colourfully that "hats flew up like corks on a surging sea." Bands played Highland airs as the couple climbed into the Glass Coach and were driven back to Buckingham Palace; the bells of the Abbey began a joyful peal which lasted for three and a half hours, and from every section of the crowd showers of confetti fluttered over the carriage, in its path and in its wake. During the eight course wedding breakfast, the traditional absence of formal speeches was respected: King George merely offered a single straightforward toast to the bride and groom, which was drunk in silence. The cake, a four-tiered

The parents of both the Duke and Duchess of York were anxious to greet them when they came back from Australasia on 27th July 1927, and the reunited family was photographed to celebrate their return. With King George V and Queen Mary (left) are the Earl and Countess of Strathmore and Kinghorne. To complete this charming group, the fifteen-month-old Princess Elizabeth sat upon her mother's knee. Though she had not seen her for six months, she had been taught to say "Mother" just in time for the Duchess' return. The tour was the first and last extensive official tour undertaken by the Yorks before their accession, and life became more patently domestic after 1927. Popular features of it were the frequent public outings for Princess Elizabeth: (right) leaving 145 Piccadilly, her parents' London home, in 1928 for a drive in Hyde Park.

affair measuring nine feet high, weighing nine hundred pounds, decorated with plaques bearing the couple's coats of arms, and festooned with sugar flowers, was cut with a silver knife and distributed among the guests who had great fun searching for seven gold charms which had been hidden in it. Lady Elizabeth, now Duchess of York as Queen Mary had been before her, received two particularly special wedding presents: one was a diamond and pearl necklace with a matching pendant from her husband, the other was the granting of the rank of Princess, conferred on her by the King during the wedding breakfast. For strangely, although according to the London Gazette she would take the style of Royal Highness "in accordance with the settled general rule that a wife takes the style of her husband" (a proposition which would come into question with the marriage in 1937 of the Duke and Duchess of Windsor), the appellation of Princess, even for the wife of a Prince, was not automatic. Nevertheless, the new Duchess took precedence as fourth lady in the land – after the Queen, Queen Alexandra and Princess Mary. The departure for the royal honeymoon was as joyful as the official marriage photographs had been solemn and wistful: the weather allowed the bride and groom to set off in an open landau, pelted with rice and confetti as they passed by the groups of family members and household staff gathered in the Palace yard to see them off and wish them God speed. Even Queen Mary relaxed sufficiently to drop a shower of rose petals from a balcony into the departing carriage.

To many wishful thinkers the marriage of the Duke of York and his demure and gentle bride sparked off a feeling of optimism in a discouraged world, and in those days they weren't afraid to say so. One fulsome, but by no means uniquely idyllic editorial

averred that it "has made us more cheerful. We have done with the long winter, spring is in the air, all Nature is astir and May Day is at hand. The outlook, both national and international, is not so bad as it seemed three months ago. *We know we are going to pull through.*"

More to the point, the marriage transformed the Duke of York's whole life every bit as much as it did for the new Duchess. Albert Duke of York was almost five years older than his twenty-two-year old wife, though if the age difference appears wide it was nothing to the contrast in their respective upbringings. Whereas hers was secure, loving, familial, his was formal, cold and unbelievably restricted. His parents, dutiful royalties though they undoubtedly were, lacked any natural parental instinct save the satisfaction of having done what was expected of them in producing children at all, and a distant pride in the limited achievements of their off-spring

"Such a relief and joy," was Queen Mary's reaction when, in the early hours of 21st April 1926, she was told of the birth of her first grand-daughter. Princess Elizabeth, known, then as now, as Lilibet to her immediate family, became a firm favourite of her royal grandparents. In particular, she delighted her mellowing grandfather, King George V, during the personal and political anxieties of his declining years, and Queen Mary, who looked after her while her parents were on tour in 1927, posed for Marcus Adams' picture (right) which was issued to celebrate the baby's first birthday. Marcus Adams also took the mother-and-daughter portrait (opposite) in July 1928, as well as the study of Princess Elizabeth in the delicate organdie party dress (far right) in 1931. By then the family had grown to four with the birth in August 1930 of Princess Margaret, and Adams' tender portrait of the Duchess with her two daughters (below), taken in 1934, became widely publicised during the years of the Silver Jubilee, accession and Coronation, as proof – if ever it was needed – of the close and loving family relationship which existed in the private world of the York household.

as they grew up. Over-impressed by the awe-inspiring dignity and unbending traditions of the later years of Queen Victoria's court, they maintained that aura of majesty and unflinching obligation throughout the more urbane years of Edward VII, and reinstated it on their own accession in 1910. Their reign had already seen the restoration of several ancient ceremonies, including the Investiture of the Prince of Wales and many refinements to Trooping the Colour, which had become almost atrophied through lack of use. By the end of World War I, in which their sense of duty twice resulted in an excess of patriotic zeal – the Palace ban on alcohol failed to catch on and the Proclamation of July 1917, by which the family and dynasty name became Windsor – they had established their style so effectively that even in the liberated, adventurous atmosphere of the 1920s no-one questioned the one British institution which growing egalitarianism should logically have begun to affect.
All this, and its aftermath which

culminated in the glorious success of the Silver Jubilee of 1935, was achieved at great cost to the King and Queen's children. Freda Dudley-Ward opined that King George V "considered them dolts, the lot of them," and Prince Albert, known in what appears to be one of the few informal parental gestures ever thrown his way as Bertie, probably got the worst of every bargain. As if in grim portent of his future, he was born on the worst possible day – 14th December, the day on which the Prince Consort in 1861, and Queen Victoria's gifted daughter Princess Alice in 1878, died and the old Queen's dread of that sorrowful anniversary was fast in the process of growing mightier by the year. Placated though she eventually was, Prince Albert, who was never a strong child, suffered from continued stomach disorders and other more common ailments and the treatment meted out by one of his earlier nurses, which included bottle-feeding while on bumpy rides in carriages, is said

The 1930s were years of fundamental change for the York family. Domestic engagements kept the parents busy, like the visit to Abercynon Colliery in Wales in June 1933 (above right), but the children soon became inevitable victims of public interest, as at the Trooping the Colour ceremony, also in June 1933 (top) when Princess Elizabeth rode with her mother, Queen Mary and the Princess Royal to Horse Guards' Parade. There were also family outings, like the visit to Glamis Castle (opposite page, bottom left) for the

presentation of colours to the Black Watch Regiment in 1935. The death of King George V on 20th January 1936 made things less easy: (top far right) the Duchess of York, recovering from influenza, arrives at Liverpool Street Station on 22nd January to join the Royal Family at Sandringham prior to the transfer of the late King's body back to London. Royal mourning did not, however, extend to the children who (opposite page, bottom right) accompanied their parents to Morning Service at Eastbourne in March 1936, and

later stood beside Queen Mary and the Duchess of York and Gloucester (opposite page, centre) after the new King had returned from the following June's Trooping the Colour ceremony. (Top right) one of the first photographs of the Duke of York after his accession; returning home to 145 Piccadilly amid great public acclaim, after dining with his brother at Fort Belvedere. Happier times (below left) as the new King and Queen joined Lord Rosebery at the Derby at Epsom in 1938.

to have rooted his life-long difficulties over his digestion. He was also fearfully nervous, much of which may have been due to his father's irascible chaffing and his mother's uncomfortably remote attitude with him, and by early childhood he was already cursed with a stammer that to one degree or another was to dog his verbal delivery throughout his life. His condition, physical and psychological, was not improved by the almost obligatory process of naval training at Dartmouth,

them which continued bachelorhood entailed. He was absolutely right to imagine that his life style was long overdue for a completely new dimension and when, shortly after his wedding, he received a letter from his father which stated that, "I am quite certain that Elizabeth will be a splendid partner in your work and share with you and help you in all you have to do," he probably read more into its significance for him than the writer had ever intended.

The marriage itself gave the Duke a new status in which he quietly revelled, and continued to revel for the ensuing twenty nine years. The Duchess brought him a contentment which had eluded him for a quarter of a century and he rarely felt better than when he was in her company. Official engagements at home assumed a lightness and a glow of success and high spirits of which they had until then been conspicuously bereft. Tours abroad became almost glamorous as crowds flocked to see this much-praised new member of the Royal Family, and when the Duchess became ill with tonsilitis during the 1927 visit to Australasia, the Duke wondered whether it would be better to cancel that part of the tour as he was sure that only through her could it be made a success. Eventually, of course, she gave him a family – a pair of

and although he showed enthusiasm his powers of learning were far from excellent, and the constant derision he received at the hands of his fellow cadets tortured him. Eventually he served in the Great War, and saw action at Jutland but all that, like much of his naval career, was constantly interrupted and eventually curtailed by his persistent poor health.

In many ways it seems remarkable that he had the psychological resilience to pursue his bride through a courtship of over two years, yet one feels instinctly that much of his persistence was born of the desperate need to release himself not only from his own family and parents but from the monotonous and possibly degrading dependence upon

Despite hasty rearrangements consequent upon King Edward VIII's abdication, the date originally fixed for his Coronation – 12th May 1937 – remained unchanged. (Left) the new King and Queen leaving Buckingham Palace in the State Coach and (below) arriving at the annexe to Westminster Abbey. Family crowns and coronets as (right), with their daughters they appeared on the balcony of Buckingham Palace, and posed afterwards for official Coronation portraits (below right). The State Coach was used again five months later for the State Opening of Parliament (opposite page, below); after the Second World War, its use for this purpose virtually ceased.

fine daughters whose attractiveness and delightfully childish antics brought their father to a peak of popularity during the last years of the old King's reign, and the era of the growing York family has long been a byword for matrimonial contentment and vicarious popular pleasure. Most of all, the Duchess determined to cure him of the impediment in his speech which several previous spells of treatment had failed to break. It was she who, late in 1926, persuaded him to have one more try when he had long since become sickened by the failure of successive specialists. Her encouragement was not merely verbal nor in any way perfunctory: she accompanied him to the Harley Street rooms of the famous Dr Lionel Logue, discussing the problem with both of them and assimilating

the details so as to be of positive assistance during the long, slow period of treatment. After only a month, he found that he had spent the last twenty-four years, as he put it, "talking the wrong way," and began the process, which he was to continue throughout his life, of learning how to do it properly and improving on each successive performance. By the time he and the Duchess left for Australia in January 1927 he was full of confidence, and throughout the succeeding years could count on his supportive and patient wife to help him to relax whilst rehearsing his speeches.

She was also the perfect antidote to his unpredictable and sometimes quite violent fits of temper – a hangover from the frustrating days of his childhood. She was able to calm him down when he began to grumble and shout, and often do so in the most delightful way. On one occasion, his ranting grew so intense that she took his hand, held his pulse and began to count quietly, fixing him with a wicked look of irreverence that even now lights up her expressive features. This made him laugh, and his anger was forgotten. The ordeal of the Abdication and his own tumultuous Accession strengthened his admiration for her positive support, and that admiration was palpable. In April 1937 Lady Diana Cooper, a guest at dinner at Windsor Castle, considered them "such a sweet little couple and so fond of each other." And when in 1947 their daughter left London for her honeymoon, he wrote a touching letter to her commending in particular his wife whom he termed "as you know, the most marvellous person in the world." The following year the King bared his soul to his people on the occasion of the Silver Wedding by confessing that "I make no secret of the fact that there have been times when my appointed task would have been almost too heavy to bear but for the strength and comfort which I have always found in my home."

Serious royal features (top) on Armistice Day, 1938 as Queen Elizabeth joined (left to right) the Duchess of Kent, Princess Helena Victoria (a grand-daughter of Queen Victoria) and Queen Mary. A return to almost Edwardian elegance characterised Cecil Beaton's portraits of the Queen in 1939 (above and opposite page, below). A family group (opposite page, top) was taken at Buckingham Palace by Marcus Adams shortly before the King and Queen's visit to Canada in April 1939, while Baron's picture of King George VI (right) celebrated the Royal Silver Wedding.

Chips Channon gave the sentiment a sharpness when, in his own diaried epitaph to King George VI in February 1952 he recalled: "He had few friends and was almost entirely dependent upon the Queen whom he worshipped: she was his willpower, his all."

The direct effect she had on him tended to cloud an important indirect benefit. When Freda Dudley-Ward described King George V's attitude to his children, she added a rider to the effect that Bertie's marriage changed it. "After that," she said, "Bertie was his favourite. He could do no wrong in his father's eyes." This profound change came about less through a re-appraisal of the son than through the attractions of the new daughter-in-law. King George, who for years fretted about the entire prospect of acquiring suitable daughters-in-law – "I hope we shall be as lucky with our daughters-in-law as Lady Holford has been: I must say I dread the idea and always have," he wrote to Queen Mary in 1922 – now found his first daughter-in-law a relaxing and disarming influence on him. They seemed to enjoy a natural

rapport, unbelievable considering the social and intellectual distance between them, but in effect stemming from her own generous understanding of the ageing monarch's need to hold on to outmoded standards of life, and a tactful respect for his servility to custom and tradition. It may not be far from the truth to say that, despite the sycophancy which surrounded them all their lives, she had correctly guessed that the King and Queen had been less than satisfactory parents and had wisely attributed their censorious and formal manner to the influence of a by-gone era. Perhaps it is a backlash against the cult of ingratiating glory which until quite recently traditionally surrounded the monarch that criticism of the likes of King George V is now so freely expressed, but in her day his senior daughter-in-law kept her criticism to herself and was as ready to charm the King as he was content to be charmed. "The better I know and the more I see of your dear little wife, the more charming I think she is and everyone falls in love with her here," he wrote to the Duke of York from Balmoral in September 1923.

He was certainly bowled over by her modest beauty and ready wit and may have detected that she did not fear him as most of his sons did. His respect for this attitude is handsomely illustrated by the famous tale, which no-one has denied, of the Duchess' late arrival for dinner one evening – a cardinal sin in the eyes of the King who, like the Queen, was promptness personified. But there was no royal castigation of the offender when she apologised for being late: "You are not late, my dear; we must all have sat down two minutes early."

In 1928 the King fell seriously ill, and the Duchess was genuinely worried about his prolonged frailty as he fought an ultimately successful battle to gain a few more years of life. His illness did not improve his impatient temper, but beneath the gruff exterior he presented she discerned a measure of kindliness and affection. When, just over seven years later, he died, she wrote to one of his doctors in terms which could

not be more touching or heartfelt. "I miss him dreadfully," she confessed. "Unlike his children I was never afraid of him and in all the twelve years of having me as a daughter-in-law he never spoke one unkind or abrupt word to me and was always ready to listen and give advice in one's own silly little affairs. He was so kind and *dependable.* And when he was in the mood, he could be deliciously funny too."

Queen Mary, who was in her mid-fifties at the time of the Yorks' wedding, was less inclined to be amused or amusing, but even her staunch, reliable, if somewhat wordly heart warmed instantly to her daughter-in-law. Shortly after the engagement she wrote to her brother, the Marquess of Cambridge, "Elizabeth is with us now, perfectly charming, so well brought up and will be a great addition to the family." Though she found in her daughter-in-law an "engaging and natural" personality, what really commended itself to Queen Mary was the history of the Bowes-Lyon family, the fascination of its ancestry and,

With the accession of King George VI and Queen Elizabeth, the young princesses, first and second in the line of succession to their father's throne, were thrust into the royal spotlight, ever-popular subjects for the news cameras on the many occasions, both private and official, when they appeared in public. (Left) at a 1938 wedding at St Margaret's, Westminster; (top) with Queen Mary at the Royal Tournament at Olympia in May 1939; (opposite page, top right) with their parents at Braemar in August 1938 and (above) at the Royal Naval College Dartmouth in 1939, where one Prince Philip of Greece was undergoing naval training.

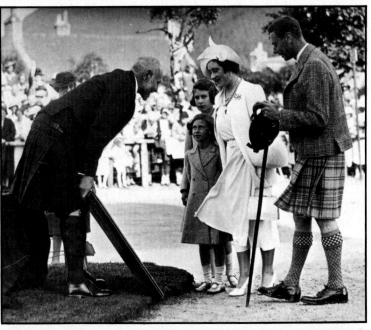

An air of fulfilment characterised the new Queen's demeanour during those brief years between the accession and the outbreak of war. It was not long before everyone echoed one eminent commentator who declared "how wholly impossible" the marriage between King Edward VIII and Mrs Simpson would have been. The Queen's classic dress sense proclaimed her enjoyment of her new métier and her wardrobe for the State Visit to France in July 1938 (left) lacked nothing in finery or style. At home, her round of duties included an inspection of new Council flats in Shoreditch in March 1938 (right) and a visit to a nursery schools display (above) at an Agricultural Show in Windsor in July 1939.

more to the point, Elizabeth's own comprehensive knowledge of history – a pursuit with which Queen Mary, steeped from her earliest years in history and royal genealogy, thoroughly sympathised. It was not lost on her, for instance, that both her son and daughter-in-law – whom she affectionately coupled in the embracing term "Bertie & E." in her diaries and personal letters – were descended from Robert the Bruce, she through his grandson Robert II, as we have seen, and he through Mary Queen of Scots.

If in these many ways the Yorks' marriage was well augured, it got off to a poor start. The young couple honeymooned at Polesden Lacey, the country house of Mrs. Ronald Greville, and set amid the pine trees and heather of the Surrey hills. It was home from home for the Duchess, who enjoyed the

leisurely first days of marriage walking the grounds and playing golf with her doting husband. But then they travelled north to Glamis where the weather turned bleak and unwelcoming, and where the Duchess caught whooping-cough – "so unromantic," wrote the Duke to his parents.

They made the best of things of course, and one of the first guests there was the Duke's elder brother the Prince of Wales. Like his parents, he was delighted with his sister-in-law, later recording that "she has brought into the family a lively and refreshing spirit." She for her part regarded him as a man of great charm and persuasion, high spirits and good intentions.

They shared a similar sense of humour, frequently twitting each other for their shortcomings, and in particular the Duchess teased him for his frequent absences on tours abroad – "you old empire-builder!" She respected him especially for his constant opposition to some of his father's more reactionary demands, and for defending his younger brothers to the best of his ability against the blasting they were liable to receive at the hands of that disciplinarian patriarch. But the Prince of Wales and the Duchess of York had quite different social attitudes, and though there was no animosity between them until the prelude to the Abdication, their social lives were led in distinctly opposite circles. After some weeks in Scotland, the honeymooners spent a few days at Frogmore on the Windsor estate before returning to London to take up residence

The Royal Tour of North America, 1939. After the six-week Canadian tour – (top right) the Queen with Canadian Prime Minister Mackenzie King in April – President Roosevelt treated his royal guests with American gusto in June. His mother Sarah sat between them (above) at the Roosevelt home in Hyde Park after morning service at St James's Church (top), while the King is seen (opposite page, far left) with the President's wife. At an earlier parade of Girl Scouts on the White House lawn, the Queen stopped her car (opposite page top) to speak to Leah Burket, who had presented a bouquet to her. Strains of Auld Lang Syne accompanied the departure of the royal train (opposite page, bottom right) at the conclusion of the visit.

at White Lodge in Richmond Park. They had chosen this delightful old house, with its commanding views over the Thames, shortly before their marriage and at the suggestion of Queen Mary whose early married life was spent there and who gave birth to her eldest son there in 1894. Previously, Queen Mary's parents occupied the house from 1869 and both died there within the following three decades. It also had associations with Queen Victoria, who spent the last summer of her marriage there with Prince Albert, reading the diaries of her late mother the Duchess of Kent, and with King George IV whose wife first occupied it as a country resort. Queen Mary, conscious of these connections, urged that the house should be kept in the family and even supervised the furnishings and decorations during the Duke and Duchess' honeymoon. On their return they watched the final stages of refurbishment, and on going

Yugoslavia, though it may have taken her some time to appreciate that her husband was the first cousin once removed of Queen Marie of Roumania, who was grandmother to the infant Prince!

It was also of course her first meeting with the Yugoslavian and Roumanian monarchs, although she had already met Prince Paul, the future Regent of Yugoslavia, and his wife

Princess Olga, sister of the future Duchess of Kent. Once again, the family reunion was a triumph for the young Duchess, whose three-day journey across Europe by train was well worth the discomfort. "They were all entranced with Elizabeth," the Duke wrote back to England; "especially cousin Missy." Missy, Queen Marie of Roumania, agreed: she found her new relative "wonderful and

into occupation in June 1923 one of their first gestures to the King and Queen was to invite them to lunch there during Ascot week. The Duchess warned them that her cooking might not be of the most advanced kind, but the royal guests were as pleased with their reception as by the happiness evident in the young couple's demeanour.

Happy as they were at home, the Duke and Duchess desperately wanted to go on tour abroad. Strangely, King George, ostensibly on the grounds that "the young people have only just been married and must settle down," refused to give them a tour of duty in the Empire at that stage. In October 1923, however, the christening of Crown Prince Peter, son of King Alexander of Yugoslavia, gave them the opportunity for a visit to the Balkans where they were to stand as god-parents or sponsors. The Duchess of York now learned at first hand some of the complexities of the genealogical link between the House of Windsor and the Karageorgevic House of

presence. No wonder the King and Queen were so unreservedly taken by their personable daughter-in-law. She had indeed slipped naturally into her public duties and had astonished friends, relatives and public alike with her sheer professionalism. Her charm extended not only to her intimates, but was capable of reaching beyond the gap which in those days habitually separated royalty from its subjects. Her flair as demonstrated in Northern Ireland was soon to be tested in distant parts of the Empire, and it says a great deal for the adaptability of the Queen Mother that, wherever and whenever she has travelled, throughout the world and through the years, she has

The Royal Family in wartime remained united, even though the young Princesses broadcast (opposite page top right) in October 1940 to encourage the evacuation of children. (Above and opposite page, top left) two Marcus Adams portraits, taken in 1941. (Top left) the Princesses with their mother at Windsor in 1940, and (left) with their father at Royal Lodge in April 1942. In 1943 the family made a rare visit to Sandringham (opposite page, bottom) where the estate had been ploughed up in collaboration with a local Agricultural Committee.

entrancing."

The Yugoslavian interlude ushered in a period of considerable travel for the Duke and Duchess which lasted for almost four years. They wintered at home in 1923/4, following the Duke's passion for the hunt by taking a short lease of a country house at Guilsborough in Northamptonshire from which they attended meets of two of the local hunts – the Pytchley and the Whaddon Chase. In July 1924 they paid an official visit to Northern Ireland, three years after the creation of the Irish State to the south, when the King himself had opened the Ulster Parliament. Despite the long history of bitterness in Irish politics, the Duke and Duchess were now accorded a reception which amazed them, and which the Duke characteristically put down to his wife's irresistible magnetism. "Elizabeth has been marvellous," he reported "and the people simply love her already. She knows exactly what to do and say to all the people we meet."

No wonder the shy, withdrawn Duke felt confident in her

invariably provoked the same warm response and infectious humour as she did on that very earliest tour.

The winter of 1924/5 gave the couple their first taste of transcontinental travel in the shape of a safari in East and North-East Africa. This was strictly a private tour, with a few official engagements – meetings with tribal chiefs etc – thrown in, and it included visits to Kenya, Uganda and the Sudan. They spent Christmas in Nairobi, the capital of Kenya which was then becoming a popular destination for Europeans in search of good hunting facilities, and both the Duke and the Duchess shot game, camping out during those expeditions which lasted several days at a time. The thought of the Queen Mother – now a lady of the gentlest leisure pursuits – shooting on safari may seem a little on the unlikely side, but in those few weeks she carried off most of the recognised trophies – rhinoceros, oryx, gazelle, water buck, steinbuck, hartebeeste, dik-dik, buffalo, water hog and jackal. In today's conservation-conscious society, that sounds a grim record but circumstances in the 1920s were

(Above) King George VI taking the Salute at a parade in 1941. (Top) the Queen meeting soldiers from a Canadian Division in April 1942: she inspected up-to-date gunnery and even rode in a Bren-gun carrier. (Left) the original royal walk-about: the King and Queen touring London on foot during the victory celebrations in May 1945. (Opposite page, top) steel helmets raised for the Royal visitors after an inspection in April 1941 of conditions at Holloway Prison in North London. One of the greatest

quite different, as was the national and international attitude to the long-established sport of aristocrats.

Within three months of their return to Britain the Duchess fell pregnant. The tidings when they were medically confirmed were circulated within the families of the prospective parents, and Princess Alice of Athlone, the mother of one of the Duchess' bridesmaids, was among the gleeful recipients. She was "thrilled to hear . . . of Elizabeth's hopes," and one can almost hear her mischievous chuckle as she added, "Kenya is famous for having that effect on people, I hear!" The news remained private until 25th November – just five days after the death of Queen Alexandra, the eighty-year-old widow of King Edward VII – though the Duchess' public appearances came to a halt long before the

supporters of the American entry into the war was Lady Astor, the American born British M.P., seen (right) with the Queen at Buckingham Palace in July 1942 after handing over a cheque for $1600 collected from American tourists to Stratford Hall, Virginia, the birthplace of Robert E. Lee. Lady Astor was also born in Virginia. (Above) the King with air crews during a tour with the Queen of bomber stations in Southern England in June 1942. Five months later he visited an aerodrome "Somewhere in England" (above right) as a guest of the United States Air Force Bomber Command by whom it had been taken over.

tell-tale signs of pregnancy could spark off any untoward comment or speculation. Unfortunately it was not, in events, an easy birth, and it was probably as well that the Duchess decided to have her child in the familiar surroundings of her parents' London home at 17 Bruton Street. Days of difficulty preceded the delivery, for which a Caesarian section was ultimately necessary. As with all births of children in close succession to the throne, the Home Secretary – in this case Sir William Joynson–Hicks – was there to ensure fair play, as far as that was compatible with the demands of propriety, and at 2.40 a.m. on 21st April 1926 the Duchess of York gave birth to a healthy girl. The King and Queen, who were awakened within an hour of the birth, now had their first grandchild in the male line, and the British public their first princess for almost thirty years – since the birth of Princess Mary in 1897. The Duke, though much gratified by his new status as a father, was full of admiration for his wife for the strength and courage she had shown in a long and difficult labour. "We always wanted a child to make our happiness complete," he wrote to Queen Mary, "and now that it has at last happened, it seems so wonderful and strange . . . I am so proud of Elizabeth at this moment after all she has gone through in the last few days . . . I know she wanted a daughter."

(Top left) Princess Elizabeth joined the Auxiliary Territorial Service in 1943. During a visit there shortly afterwards, the King, Queen and Princess Margaret saw her at work (top right) in the Motor Transport Section. (Right) the King at a working lunch with Generals Patton and Clark during a tour of United States armed forces in June 1943 and (far right) with General Eisenhower, Supreme Commander in Western Europe, while visiting fighting fronts in France in October 1944, when the campaign to liberate France was well under way. (Above) the King and Queen leaving St Paul's Cathedral after a service in 1943.

(Right) the King meeting an army padre at an inspection of an Airborne Division in May 1944, shortly before the invasion of France in which it was to take part. The Queen and Princess Elizabeth look on. (Below) the first investiture of its kind: the King knights Sir Francis Linnell (deputy AOC in the Middle East) during a tour of forces in North Africa in February 1943. (Below right) the Queen, escorted by Ernest Bevin, inspecting American ambulance drivers in the courtyard of Buckingham Palace in June 1943. (Bottom) the Queen – a maple leaf badge in her hat – with Canadian soldiers in camouflage gear, in April 1942.

And so the lady who now wears Britain's crown as Queen Elizabeth II came into the world. Had the world known then what it knows now it may have made a great deal more of the event than it did. As it was, the possibility of the Prince of Wales marrying and producing Britain's future sovereigns seemed as strong as ever, and the event which delighted the Yorks now elicited a public response that was curious and kindly rather than festive and celebratory. Within a fortnight the country was plunged into its first and only General Strike and there was plenty of other, harder news to exercise the minds of its citizens. Shortly after the strike

The question arose early as to the child's names and the Duke felt it incumbent on himself to seek his father's approval for the choice of Elizabeth (after her mother) Alexandra (after her late great-grandmother) Mary (after her grandmother). "I am sure," confided the Duke, "that there will be no muddle over two Elizabeths in the family. We are so anxious for her first name to be Elizabeth as it is such a nice name." The King agreed that it was "a very pretty name," but wrote to Queen Mary that "Bertie says nothing about Victoria" – an allusion to Queen Victoria's insistence that all her female descendents should bear her name. No doubt much to the Yorks' relief, the King added, "I hardly think that necessary."

ended, the month-old Princess Elizabeth was christened at Buckingham Palace by Archbishop Lang, and the first of a series of delightful photographs was released, taken by Marcus Adams, the man whose portraits of her charted her growth into adolescence and the childhood of her own children in the early 1950s. Princess Elizabeth of York was barely nine months old when her parents were at last granted their original wish to go on tour: King George V decided that a visit to Australia and New Zealand would be appropriate. The timing may well have seemed rather perverse in view of what we now recognise as the necessity for bonding between mother and child, particularly as in those days, unlike the present,

there was never any question of
the royal visitor being able to
take her baby along with her.
The Duchess' home instincts
did in fact get the better of her
for a time, and she found the
parting from her beloved baby
daughter too much. "I felt very
much leaving on Thursday," she
wrote back to Queen Mary
shortly after sailing from
Portsmouth on 27th January
1927, "and the baby was so
sweet playing with the buttons
on Bertie's uniform that it quite
broke me up." Indeed, rumour
has it that the car which took the
Duke and Duchess to Victoria
Station had to circle Grosvenor
Gardens a couple of times to
allow the Duchess to compose
herself for the public farewells.

The royal tour itself, the only
major official one they made
before their accession almost ten
years later, was a monumental
success, all the more so in the
light of the Duke's uneasy
feeling that he was very much a
second-rate royal visitor by
comparison with his elder
brother who had captivated the
Australians and New Zealanders
during his much-publicised tour
a few years before. How well the
Duke would have done in his
own right may only now be
guessed at, but it was certain
that with his wife by his side the
enterprise could not fail. The
Australians, even if less hard-
bitten then than they might be
considered today, found her
irresistible and "fell in love with
her" while in New Zealand an
expatriate Scotsman wrote that
"she shines and warms like

noted Communist sympathiser whose loyalties changed the moment he saw the Duchess. "They're human!" he had declared. "Yesterday I was in the crowd with my wife, and one of the children waved his hand. I'm blessed if the Duchess didn't wave back and smile right into my face not two yards away. I'll never say a word against them again: I'm done with it for good and all."

The Duchess' heavy programme of duties was relieved by the occasional rest day, and she did

The cessation of hostilities in Europe led to a brief moment of jubilation, and the Royal Family's appearance on the balcony of Buckingham Palace (opposite page, top) on 8th May 1945 epitomised the sense of deliverance. That August they were cheered to and from St Paul's Cathedral (below) for a thanksgiving service following the Japanese surrender. In June 1946, a massive Victory Parade combined celebration with tribute to the many troops newly returned from abroad. Queen Mary, then in her 80th year, was a

sunlight." Back home, there were parliamentary rumblings when two Labour M.P.s described the visit as a "pleasure trip," deploring in terms of facile abuse the expense involved at a time of industrial depression. King George V took this as a personal insult against his family, and resented having them set up as targets for left-wing derision. He maintained, stalwartly as he always did in his occasional *contre-temps* with Parliament, that "as long as the monarchy and the Empire exist, it is but natural that the Dominions should look for periodic visits from members of the Royal Family." At the same time the criticism prompted him to set the precedent preventing any such visits from taking place unless the host nation footed the bill.

The Duke and Duchess were not unaware of this dispute, but they had a job to do. They did it well too, by all accounts. The New Zealand Prime Minister reported that he had met a

proud onlooker as the tanks and battalions filed past (opposite page, bottom). Sadly, President Roosevelt, a staunch ally from the earliest days of the war, did not survive to see its successful conclusion: his death from cancer led the Royal Family once again to St Paul's for his memorial service in April 1945 (left). Two years later, London celebrated as Princess Elizabeth, now 21, married her third cousin, formerly Prince Philip of Greece in Westminster Abbey (above left). Princess Margaret was chief bridesmaid and appeared on the Palace balcony (opposite page, centre) with her parents and grandmother.

a spot of trout fishing – a pastime which in its various forms she has enjoyed ever since, whether in the lakes of New Zealand or in the River Dee near Birkhall. Her bout of tonsillitis lasted for ten days, after which the Duke was relieved to have her back with him for the remaining part of the tour. Everyone – the royal visitors, the host nations, the King and Queen and the public – considered the tour an unqualified success, and in the most persuasive way it gave the lie to the Prince of Wales' famous deprecation fifteen years before: "What rot and a waste of time, money and energy all these State Visits are!"

Domestic issues took a hold on their return to Britain that spring, when the Duke and Duchess took a ten-year Crown lease on a house in Piccadilly. White Lodge, for all its cosy family ambience, was found to be too large, too expensive to run, too inconvenient for the many journeys up to London each week, and too vulnerable to the legitimate but unwelcome curiosity of crowds of day-trippers to Richmond Park. The Prince of Wales, who visited his

old birth-place shortly after his brother and sister-in-law went into occupation, had been appalled by its lack of comfort, in spite of the installation of electricity and new bathrooms. The new home, a four-storeyed grey-stone house known as 145 Piccadilly, was in a far more accessible position where the public was concerned, but at the same time a less likely target for snooping from passers-by, most of whom were far too busy going about their own everyday business, and it was here that its royal occupants spent some of the most peaceful and contented years of their joint lives as a close family unit. Now long ago demolished, the memory of 145 Piccadilly is as golden to the daughters of the family as those halcyon days at Glamis and St Paul's were to the Duchess

herself.
For by the end of the decade, a second daughter had joined the growing clan. The emphasis on royal domesticity was strengthened by the news early in 1930 that the Duchess was again with child, and as if to

reaffirm to the Royal Family's recent connections with the Strathmores, it was decided that the birth should take place at Glamis Castle where the Duchess' parents, now in advancing years, were thrilled with the honour of her choice. It

Queen Elizabeth II's early official portraits. (Opposite page, top) two by Dorothy Wilding, taken in 1952. The Queen's necklace, in the left hand photograph, was a wedding present from the Nizam of Hyderbad. (Opposite page, bottom) with the Duke of Edinburgh, Admiral of the Fleet, in Baron's portrait released January 1954: the Queen's tiara and brooch were wedding gifts from Queen Mary. (Above) a happy portrait by Baron, published in April 1953,

showing the Queen wearing Queen Victoria's diamond diadem and a Russian fringe diamond necklace presented to her by the City of London. (Top left) another Baron study, released to mark the State Visit to France in April 1957: the Queen's diamond and emerald tiara and necklace once belonged to Queen Mary. (Left) Canadian photographer Donald McKeague's portrait of the Queen and Prince Philip, issued May 1959.

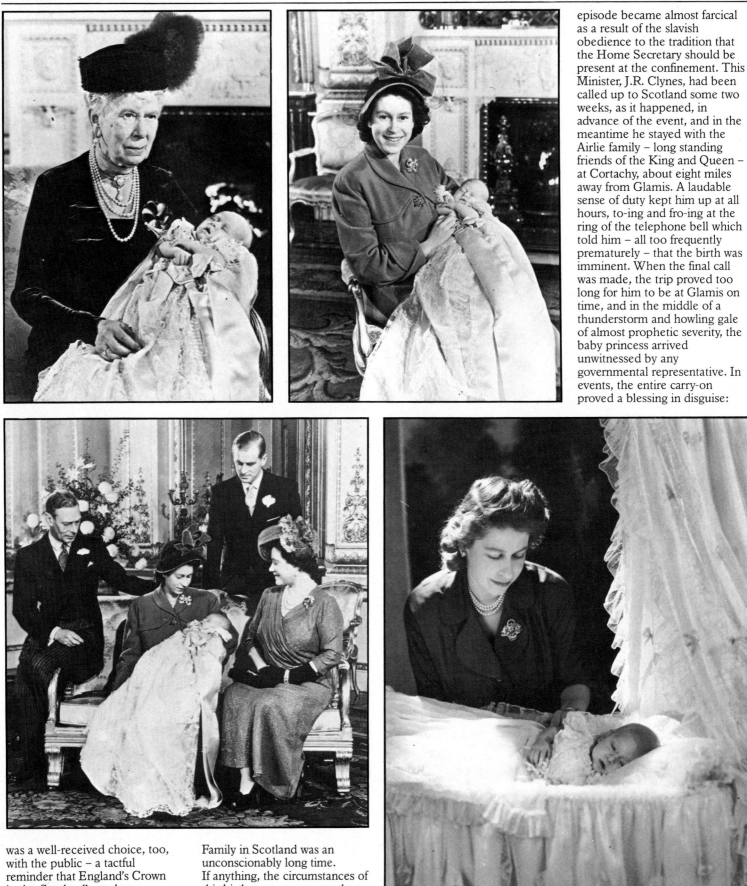

episode became almost farcical as a result of the slavish obedience to the tradition that the Home Secretary should be present at the confinement. This Minister, J.R. Clynes, had been called up to Scotland some two weeks, as it happened, in advance of the event, and in the meantime he stayed with the Airlie family – long standing friends of the King and Queen – at Cortachy, about eight miles away from Glamis. A laudable sense of duty kept him up at all hours, to-ing and fro-ing at the ring of the telephone bell which told him – all too frequently prematurely – that the birth was imminent. When the final call was made, the trip proved too long for him to be at Glamis on time, and in the middle of a thunderstorm and howling gale of almost prophetic severity, the baby princess arrived unwitnessed by any governmental representative. In events, the entire carry-on proved a blessing in disguise:

was a well-received choice, too, with the public – a tactful reminder that England's Crown is also Scotland's, and an acknowledgement that the three-and-a-quarter centuries which had passed since the last birth of a member of the Royal Family in Scotland was an unconscionably long time. If anything, the circumstances of this birth were even worse than when Princess Elizabeth was born four years earlier. Not only was another Caesarean section necessary, but the whole

The birth of Prince Charles marked another regenerative milestone in the Royal Family's history, and the photographs after his christening on 15th December 1948 illustrate its dynastic significance. Mother (left), grandmother (right) and great-grandmother (far left) held the new baby, while the family group (opposite page, bottom left) showed the King for the first time since his treatment for arteriosclerosis. Prince Charles' first official portrait with Princess Elizabeth (opposite page, bottom right) was also published in December 1948, and a further photograph, with both parents, followed early the next year (below).

using it as the perfect illustration of the indignity and waste of energies which this outdated ritual could entail, the Duke, as King George VI, dispensed with it when his elder daughter gave birth to her first child, the present Prince of Wales, in 1947. Perpetuating the Scottish flavour of this latest royal event, they called the new princess Margaret, and added Rose as a tribute to the Duchess' favourite flower. She had initially wanted to call the baby Ann Margaret – she liked the sound of Ann of York – but for once King George V was against. So Ann was dropped, resurrected, with an additional "e," almost exactly twenty years later with the birth of the present Queen's daughter. In November 1947, King George VI proudly wrote to Princess Elizabeth, "I have watched you grow up all these years under the skilful direction of Mummy," and both as Duchess of York and later as Queen Elizabeth "Mummy" assumed overall charge and supervision of the upbringing of both her daughters. She brought into the nursery a succession of Scottish nannies and governesses to take her place while public duty called her from home, and their sheer quality prompted many members of the Royal Family to look to Scots for their nursery staff. Among them, Clara Cooper-Knight was the original old retainer from Glamis days, and Marion Crawford – "Crawfie" to the Princesses – worked long, hard and successfully to emulate her. The Royal children grew up in close camaraderie, despite the four-year age difference, thanks largely to their mother's insistence that Princess Elizabeth should neither resent the attentions understandably accorded to the younger sister nor patronise her. They took

many of their lessons together in the privacy of Buckingham Palace or one or other of their parents' country homes, but their mother also arranged for them to be taught to play the piano, took them to dancing classes at Vacani's in the West End and stimulated their interest and proficiency in the French language by encouraging French conversation at home to supplement their daily lessons. She did not however push them educationally – merely encouraging them to do their best, and if Princess Elizabeth failed to shine at maths – well, that was the way of things. Generally she followed her own lights in establishing guide-lines for the moral, social and physical welfare of her daughters – open air, as much country life as possible, responsible manners, good deportment and all the social graces comprised the priorities. In addition of course, she was in an undoubtedly

enviable position to see that they could be present at all the great seasonal events in London and indeed throughout the country – the Royal Tournament, Trooping the Colour, the Silver Jubilee, country shows at Windsor, the Braemar Gathering, garden parties at Glamis, and so on.

What the Duchess was most concerned about, certainly until she became Queen and the whole family was catapulted into unrelenting publicity, was to protect her daughters from the worst excesses of public curiosity. By the time Princess Margaret was a toddler, the belief was beginning to spread that marriage was not for the Prince of Wales, and that in the Duke of York's family lay the future crowned heads of Britain. Consequently there was an insatiable demand for photographs of the growing children, particularly in the mid-1930s when the marriages of

King George's remaining sons boosted the family image even further, and by 1936 a five-minute newsreel was available showing the Duke and Duchess with their children cheerfully at play with bat and ball, corgis at their feet, running amongst the daffodils, and altogether projecting that healthy, recognisable family atmosphere which did so well for them the following year. Nevertheless the Duchess had her periodic doubts: as early as 1929 she detected a great disappointment

(Below) the King, Queen and Princess Margaret driving through London after the Silver Wedding thanksgiving service at St Paul's in April 1948. The occasion was

marked by official portraits by Baron (previous pages), and Cecil Beaton's portrait of the Queen (also overleaf) was taken in the same year. (Right) the Queen arriving at the People's Palace to see Shaw's In Good King Charles' Golden Days in October 1948, and (far right) with Princess Margaret and the Duke of Edinburgh at the Empire, Leicester Square, for the Royal Film Performance that November. (Opposite page) Princesses Elizabeth and Margaret arriving at the London Coliseum for a performance of Humpty Dumpty in January 1949. (Top pictures) Beaton's studies of Princess Elizabeth with Prince Charles and Princess Anne in the sitting room of Clarence House in September 1950.

among the Scots when she visited Edinburgh without taking Princess Elizabeth with her, and commented, "It almost frightens me that people should love her so much. I suppose that is a good thing . . ."

The setting for much of the Yorks' home life in the early 1930s was a newly-acquired country house in Windsor Great Park, called Royal Lodge, and if there was ever a favourite retreat for the present Queen Mother, this was it. Over half a century after she and her husband took it over, it is probably the house closest to her heart as the residence essentially of her own choice. Buckingham Palace of course went with the job on their accession in 1936, Clarence House – delightful though it is – was forced on her by widowhood, Sandringham now belongs to her elder daughter, but Royal Lodge Windsor, though in strictness the property of the reigning sovereign, is the Queen Mother's precious week-end haven for life.

A nation strengthened in its affection towards the monarchy by the experience of war could not see enough of the Royal Family, whose life was almost daily chronicled in pictures. Major royal occasions continued apace, from the Festival of Britain – (opposite page, top right) the Queen and Queen Mary greeting Prince Michael of Kent in May 1951 – to Princess Elizabeth's visit to North America – (below) greeted by President Truman in Washington that November. Royal birthdays came thick and fast. Pictures at Balmoral (left and opposite page, bottom right) were taken on Princess Margaret's 21st birthday in August 1951; Marcus Adams was still there to take Princess Anne's first birthday pictures (opposite page) the same month, and Prince Charles' third birthday in November became memorable for what is now one of his own favourite photographs (bottom left): the King-to-be with his grandfather, to whom less than three months of life remained.

The Duke and Duchess had to ask for it of course, but King George V had no hesitation in allowing them to take it over. It was not a difficult decision, judging by the deplorable condition in which they found it: unoccupied for almost a century, it was last lived in by King William IV, and Queen Victoria paid many happy visits to her bluff old uncle there when she was a young girl. But even he had much of the original fabric torn down, and by the time the Yorks came across it, it was in a disheartening state of neglect, unloved by anyone, utterly derelict. But its new owners saw its potential, and with the Duke's vision for landscape gardening and the Duchess' passion for flowers, it was not long before they began to transform what then passed for a garden, while the interior and exterior of the house itself underwent complete renovation.

high, from which one could look through any one of five massive windows onto the terrace, the lawns and the peaceful backdrop of woodlands. The Queen Mother's day-room – called the Octagon Room – now houses her handsome writing desk with its clutter of books, papers, family photographs and, of course, a vase or two of flowers, and from which while working there she can gaze onto an attractive paved herb garden.

It was to this house, distinctive to all comers to this south-east corner of the park by the warm pink wash which graces its outer walls – strawberries and cream, someone called it – that the Duke and Duchess brought their children in 1933, and which became the focus of their family life up to, through and even after the second World War. By the

This was a labour of love, and many successive weekends and holidays were spent by the couple personally clearing large areas of rhododendron-tangled undergrowth and beating back swathes of nettles and weeds. Visitors who dropped by to witness the proceedings were liable to be press-ganged into service themselves, and before long a substantial area of the garden was ready for planting. This was carried out under the expert supervision of Sir Eric Savill, who became a good friend of the Yorks and whose name now graces another garden – which any member of the public can now see – laid out over twenty acres in another part of Windsor Park. At his suggestion, woodland walks were marked out, winding between rhododendron and azalea bushes, and dominated by two huge cedar trees close to the house itself; herbaceous borders took shape, a sunken garden was developed and, especially for the Duchess, a copy of the statue of Charity, the original of which was and is at St Paul's Walden Bury, was placed at the end of one of the high-hedged allées – themselves a reminder of her childhood garden in Hertfordshire.

The house was completely stripped down and the interior redesigned to include a huge salon of a thousand square feet, with walls almost thirty feet time Princess Margaret was eight, an open-air swimming pool had been added, but perhaps the enduringly delightful addition to the grounds was the little house "Y Bwthyn Bach" which the people of Wales presented to Princess Elizabeth on her tenth birthday, just three months after the death of her grandfather King George V. It is the perfect picture book country cottage in miniature, refined in every detail of its reflection of the contemporary ideal in design. Nestling close to Royal Lodge itself, standing fifteen feet high and containing all the household items and furnishings one would expect to find in a building of its type in any part of the country, it represents a cross between a large doll's house and a full-sized cottage, between

ornamentation and utility – a small scale variation in concept and design on the Swiss Cottage which Queen Victoria had built in the grounds of Osborne House as an educational and recreational retreat for her large family. As such, it has delighted three generations of royal children already as it will no doubt continue to delight others. Its present guardian is the Queen Mother's junior grand-daughter, Lady Sarah Armstrong-Jones.

The Duchess was always welcome at Glamis Castle, of course – the people of Glamis

In March 1951 the Queen visited the Royal Horticultural Society's Orchid Show at Westminster (opposite page, top); in May she joined the King at Westminster Abbey for the Order of the Bath service (above right) and seemed cheerful at the Derby (opposite page, bottom right). June saw her welcoming King Haakon of Norway on a State Visit to Britain (left), and in October she saw the Royal Variety Performance at the Victoria Palace (opposite page, bottom left). In November she attended the wedding of her niece, Mary Bowes-Lyon, at Smithfield (above) and was at Westminster Abbey again for a WVS memorial service (right).

have always been possessive about her and treated her as their own – and her father and mother kept perpetual open house for her and her family. But, being the youngest daughter, she always appreciated that the Castle would never be hers by right and so shortly after acquiring Royal Lodge Windsor she and her husband began to look for their own home in Scotland. They found it in the shape of Birkhall in Aberdeenshire, an old Queen Anne building which served as a dower house to the Balmoral Estate, and which lies snugly against the pine-forested hillside only eight miles from Prince Albert's Balmoral Castle. By it runs the River Dee, where the Duchess took up salmon fishing and has continued this absorbing pastime almost up to the present day, and Loch Muick, on which more royal sailors first took to their boats than anywhere else, ripples peacefully close by. As with Royal Lodge, the Duke and Duchess decided it needed alterations inside and out: two wings were immediately added and its cottage garden was

developed to match the character of the house itself, with its dormer windows and its quaint old staircase leading up to the back door.

Thus, by the middle of the decade, the young Princesses were able to spend their innocent childhood, one which the present Queen is said to have described as "a time when the sun always seemed to be shining" moving regularly between their London home in Piccadilly, Royal Lodge Windsor and Birkhall, with additional invited holidays at Balmoral and Sandringham. For them the quality of life was exquisite, particularly in the long, despairing days of the Depression, and their parents were able to look contentedly upon their privileged existence which all too soon would be paid for by the unexpected, unwanted burden of intense and continuing public duty.

Their grandfather's reign enjoyed a high summer in the mid 1930s. The wedding in 1934 of the Duke of Kent to the almost ethereally beautiful Princess Marina of Greece and, a year later, of the Duke of

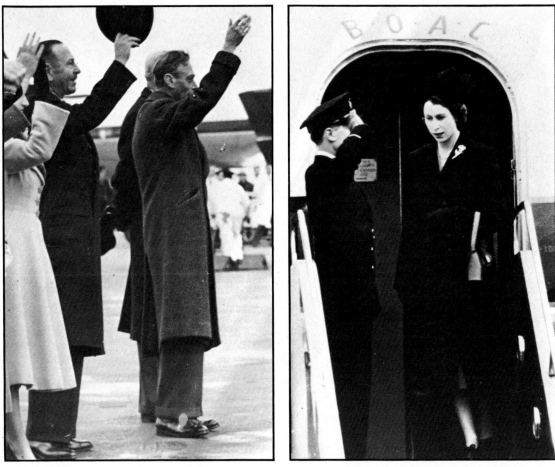

Gloucester to an attractive, quiet and very English Alice Montagu-Douglas-Scott provided the prelude and coda to the glorious triumph of King George V's Silver Jubilee celebrations in May 1935. Britain, gradually easing herself out of the worst of a catastrophic world-wide recession, relished these successive festivities almost as evidence that things were getting better. The sight of crowds lining routes or surging before the railings of Buckingham Palace became commonplace – almost a cult – and the Yorks, with their engaging, bubbly children frequently dressed cutely in matching clothes, enjoyed great popularity.

One Socialist denounced these continuing royal celebrations as "aspirins for a sick society," but in fact it was the seventy-year-old King who, the family were about to discover, was a very sick man. On Christmas Day in 1935 he made his fourth and last broadcast of his annual Christmas message with a delivery noticeably more gravelly and laboured than

On 31st January 1952 the King, with the Queen and Princess Margaret, stood on the tarmac at Heathrow Airport (above) to see Princess Elizabeth and her husband off on a Commonwealth tour which he himself was too ill to make. Chips Channon wrote, "I . . . saw the King, bare-headed, cross, almost mad-looking, waving farewell to the Edinburghs, who have flown to Kenya en route for Australia. He is reported to be going out duck-shooting next week – suicidal." His prophecy was almost suspiciously accurate: the King died in his sleep on 6th February after a day shooting hares at Sandringham. His widow, soon to be known as Queen Elizabeth, the Queen Mother, was the first to be informed and Princess Elizabeth, recalled from Africa, met her Cabinet and Privy Counsellors (right) at the foot of the aircraft which on 7th February brought her back onto British soil as Queen. Londoners reflected the nation's bewilderment (opposite page, bottom right) as newspapers spread the news, and for two solemn minutes on 15th February, the day of the King's funeral, the whole of London came willingly to a respectful standstill (opposite page, bottom left).

before – even for his deeply resonant and gutteral voice. Weighed down by sheer old age and unrelieved by the effects of constantly heavy smoking, his familiar features became etched with exhaustion, and his last New Year holiday at Sandringham saw him despairing from the onset of his final, mercifully short illness. By 16th January 1936 an anxious Queen Mary summoned her sons to their father's bedside, though the Duchess of York was herself suffering badly from pneumonia and influenza and was unable to accompany her husband to Sandringham. There were few rallies of any significance and by the 18th most realistic hope was gone. His progress towards inevitable death was marked by bulletins of which the most famous – "the King's life is moving peacefully towards its close" – was penned by his grieving wife. The story goes that shortly before his death on 20th January, he

received news in his half slumbering state that at Park House only half a mile away, the wife of his friend Lord Fermoy had just given birth to a daughter. The dying King would have relished the coincidence that the new-born girl was to become the mother of Diana Princess of Wales whose son, Prince William would be

christened on the 82nd birthday of none other than Elizabeth Duchess of York.

A long and strictly-observed period of mourning for her dead father-in-law gave the Duchess of York little opportunity to consider, far less play herself into, her new circumstances before the enervating events of 1936 began to overwhelm her.

The first four weeks were effectively written off as she struggled to throw off the persistent and debilitating effects of the severe bout of influenza which had kept her away from Sandringham during the King's last illness, and when she recovered it was to find things eerily different. Just as in 1901 the then Duchess of York, later

Queen Mary, had deplored the prospect of "England without the Queen (Victoria)" so the loss of another well-loved sovereign in 1936 seemed to cause the present Duchess a strange and unexplained feeling of unease. "Everything is different," she wrote in March 1936 to Lord Dawson of Penn, "especially spiritually and mentally . . . I mind things that I don't like, more than before." This statement has never been authoritatively expanded upon but it has become almost renowned for its prophetic content, in view of the turmoils which the immediate future held.

At the time of her marriage the possibility of her bridegroom ever becoming King must have seemed remote enough. Now thirteen years had slipped away and the old sovereign's death left a middle-aged bachelor as monarch. The fear must have trespassed across the Duke of York's thoughts that the new King might remain a bachelor, or at best marry someone for whom, being of similar years, childbearing was undesirable or medically inadvisable. As for the Duchess, she might have chilled, had she known of it then, to the recollection of George V's hope that his eldest son would never marry and that "nothing will

On 11th February 1952 the mortal remains of King George VI, like his father before him, were brought back to London for the ritual of the Lying-in-State: (right) the simple procession leaving King's Cross Station for Westminster Hall, where (opposite page) the three Queens waited to pay their public respects at a short service. Four days later the royal coffin was removed to Windsor, borne through the streets of London – Piccadilly (far right), Green Park (below right) and Edgware Road (below) – to Paddington Station (bottom) where a train waited (previous page) to convey it to Windsor for the funeral and committal at St George's Chapel.

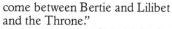

come between Bertie and Lilibet and the Throne."

With the benefit of hindsight the Duchess might have regarded the alternative, and very real, possibility with greater aversion. There can be little doubt that the name of Wallis Simpson was too often mentioned in London Society for it to be unknown to members of the Royal Family, nor that the lady's ready fame owed everything to her popularity with the new King. As Prince of Wales, he had met her at a country house in Leicestershire five years before and, following his usual penchant for married women, had formed a barely concealed but, in the quaint and rather hypocritical circumstances in which high society then functioned, respectable liaison. There is evidence that King George V knew of it and feared the inevitable development into a prospect of marriage and its

potential for creating trouble, and both he and his heir harboured independent intentions to discuss the matter together. For various reasons, eminently understandable in the light of their uncertain and almost distrustful relationship, the problem remained unspoken of until, months after the parent's demise, it began to surface beyond further concealment. By October 1936, all those most closely concerned were in no doubt that the King wished to marry his constant

companion and that, it was constitutionally impossible for her, twice divorced – as by the end of that month she was – and with both husbands living, to be crowned consort to a King pledged to defend a faith which abhorred and shunned divorce. It is unlikely that the Duchess of York envisaged anything remotely approaching her brother-in-law's abdication when, in the Spring of 1936, she and the Duke visited him, at Fort Belvedere – the visit would otherwise almost certainly not

have taken place particularly as one of the King's guests at the time was Mrs Simpson herself. This is the first recorded encounter between the two future sisters-in-law and there was suspicion from the start: Mrs Simpson noticed, with her usual ready perception, that the Duchess "was not sold" on the King's "American interest." The hour-long meeting was not followed up until early that July when the new King gave a

Even Coronation year brought sadness when, on 24th March, Queen Mary died aged 84. The Queen Mother, who drove to Marlborough House that evening (top left) was one of the last to see her. More cheerfully, she attended a Colonial garden party at Lambeth Palace in June (above) before leaving with Princess Margaret for Rhodesia (far left). Back in London in August, she attended a service for the Friends of St Paul's (left) – she is still their Patron. (Opposite) her daughter and grandchildren, photographed by Marcus Adams late in 1953.

dinner party at York House, St. James's Palace, where both Mrs Simpson and the Yorks were amongst the guests. Again, what contact occurred was cool and it is generally reckoned to be consequent upon this event that mutual dislike between the two ladies germinated. Matters were not improved by the knowledge that Mrs Simpson was acting as hostess during the King's stay at Balmoral where he busied himself entertaining society friends on a grand scale – this to the consternation of Queen Mary, who was much put out by the conspicuous absence, for want of royal invitation, of the usual Establishment figures – nor by several other examples of the King's waywardness, the most famous being the cancellation of an official engagement in Aberdeen, ostensibly on grounds of mourning, but in reality affording the opportunity for him to greet Mrs Simpson personally after her long train journey to Balmoral.

Indeed, by the time King Edward plucked up sufficient courage to inform Queen Mary

of his intentions it appears that nothing short of revulsion could adequately describe the attitude of the ladies of the Royal Family towards the *parvenue* Mrs Simpson. To the Duchess of York this was an almost alien sentiment, appreciable not in the context of personal outlook on life, but only by reference to her sheer unbelieving horror of the consequences the looming crisis could bring. Wisely, tactfully, she

The splendour of the Coronation was unparalleled in British social history, television helping to translate its mysteries into the significance of royal commitment. The streets of London were thick with crowds as the Queen rode in the State Coach to Westminster Abbey via Trafalgar Square (below). She returned home smiling and carrying her regalia into Buckingham Palace (left). (Opposite page) the Queen with her Mistress of the Robes and six Maids of Honour (top), and with her many British and foreign relatives (bottom) in this largest European royal gathering since the war.

chose not to take any initiative in influencing her brother-in-law's actions, despite their mutual characteristics and the respect and even companionship she had always felt for him, but her residual sympathy and even

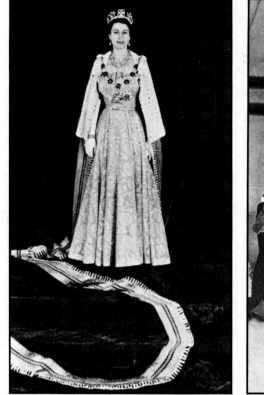

Scenes from Queen Elizabeth II's Coronation in June 1953. (Opposite page) her arrival at Westminster Abbey with the Duke of Edinburgh. (Far right) preparation for her Anointing: a canopy of cloth-of-gold, carried by four Knights of the Garter, shields the Queen from all eyes as, stripped of jewellery and fine robes, and clad only in a simple white dress, she awaits this private ritual. (Below) the moment of Coronation: the Queen wearing St Edward's Crown and carrying the Rod and Sceptre is surrounded by her bishops and coronetted peers. (Right) the Queen in the Throne Room of Buckingham Palace after her first State Opening of Parliament on 4th November 1952.

affection for him was drained by the indecent speed and obvious resolution with which he alienated himself from her and her husband. As the King had not found voice with his father on the general matter of his personal feelings so he could not, or would not, keep his

In the 1950s, the Queen Mother resumed a heavy programme of official duties. During a trip to Canada in autumn 1954 she paid a short visit to New York, as guest of honour at the Columbia University Charter Day dinner at the Waldorf Astoria (bottom right). After her return she attended, with Princess Margaret, a fashion show at Carlton House Terrace, and was greeted (below) by her own fashion designer, Norman Hartnell. (Right) the Queen Mother receiving a bouquet from Clarissa Watson at the Royal Naval College Greenwich, where she opened the Queen Elizabeth II ante-room June 1955.

family – not even his immediate successor – informed of the complex and ever-changing events which led up to the explosion of public information early in December, when the British Press finally ended the strange interlude of its self-imposed silence on the subject of what then became universally known as "The King's Marriage."

Consequently neither the Duke nor the Duchess was aware that the storm had broken until, emerging from Euston Station after an overnight journey from Scotland where, during five days' engagements, the Duchess had been given the Freedom of the City of Edinburgh, their eyes lighted not only upon the huge crowd gathered outside but also upon the billboards which effectively proclaimed the reason for such unusual public interest in their arrival. The Duke's face dropped in bewilderment, and for once the Duchess' famous smile failed to materialise. In a state of utter dismay – "surprised and horrified" in the Duke's own words – they both made for Buckingham Palace where ten days of arguments and recrimination in the bosom of

Britain's most famous family began.

By all accounts, and understandably, it was a time of profound shock. With Queen Mary still grieving in early widowhood and dependent upon the support of her only daughter the Princess Royal, and with the Duke of York shattered under the mounting pressure of an inexorable destiny, it fell to the Duchess to lead the prolonged and, in events, hopeless attack

(Opposite page, top right) the Queen Mother with Prince Charles and Princess Anne at a Meet of the West Norfolk Hunt at Hillingdon, near Sandringham, in January 1956. (Top left) inspecting a Royal Scottish Regiment guard of honour in August 1956, when she received the freedom of Musselburgh, in Midlothian. (Left) meeting a male nurse at a concert in St James's Palace in aid of the Queen's Institute of District Nursing in December 1954. (Above) opening the Governesses' Benevolent Institution's new home at Chislehurst in July 1955.

against the King. The play *Crown Matrimonial* which enjoyed a lengthy success on the stage and television in the mid 1970s cast the Duchess as the dominant adversary to King Edward, berating him for his lack of judgement, the inept handling of the issue and, above all, for keeping all his family so totally uninformed. That last score at least is well supported by evidence. Like her husband, the Duchess of York was angered at the seemingly systematic way in which the King avoided all attempts to be contacted by his brother until most of the vital decisions had effectively been made. The Duke of York finally forced a meeting, but not before the Duchess, blazing with frustration, had complained, "Everyone knows more than we

The Queen Mother's grandson at work and play. (Right) a 1956 birthday portrait by Antony Armstrong-Jones. (Bottom right) back to Hill House School, Knightsbridge, after the Easter holidays, May 1957. (Below) Badminton, 1960, with mother, sister and aunt, the Princess Royal.

do. We know nothing! Nothing!"
In the meantime she, like her royal relations had to cope with her usual round of public engagements and, domestically, with the natural inquisitiveness of her two children. To them

(Right) Prince Charles and Princess Anne at the Royal Windsor Horse Show in May 1958. (Opposite page, bottom left) the Queen Mother's new grandson, Prince Andrew, on his first family summer holiday at Balmoral in 1960. Secondary education awaited the elder brother who, in April 1962 (below) was shown around his new school, Gordonstoun.

and to members of her retinue she maintained an outward air of wistful resignation: "We must take what's coming to us, and make the best of it," she told Miss Crawford, the Princesses' governess. On other occasions her indignation bordered on contempt: before the year was out she affirmed bitterly, "None of this would have happened if Wallis hadn't blown in from Baltimore!"

By the early afternoon of 11th December 1936 everything *had* happened. Parliament gave effect to the Abdication Act, and in giving the Royal Assent to it, King Edward VIII ceased to be an Empire's sovereign. He was even then preparing his final broadcast to the nation before leaving for France. In his place, by automatic succession, the Duke of York assumed the throne and his Duchess, now Queen, entered the Litany of the Church of England for the first time. Perversely she was laid low with influenza at 145 Piccadilly, ending the year much as she had started it, and she was unable to

be present as the Royal Family bid tearful, incredulous farewells to the departing ex-King at Windsor. Instead, she sent him a letter, which he read in the car which took him to Portsmouth Dockyard. Despite the past weeks' bitterness, its contents were probably devoid of unfair reproach: the character of the writer suggests the possibility; the kindly message "Hope Elizabeth better" in the exile's first telegram from France the following morning seems to clinch it.

On 12th December the Duke of York attended his Accession Council, declaring that he would be known as George VI, and that his brother would take the title Duke of Windsor. Thus a Duke became King, a King became a Duke and for the first time since the Norman Conquest three adult Kings had sat upon England's throne in the same year. But that was really only the beginning of the Abdication story and what followed has provided much of the Western world with periods of voyeuristic fascination as Britain's first family attempted to cope with the *débris* of the crisis. The tale is an unedifying one, pregnant with machination, accusation and cross-purpose. The country had come closer than most were then prepared to admit to division into factions and it was perhaps only the swift, almost clinical departure of Edward VIII which saved it from damage in the hour of crisis. But the situation had to be consolidated, particularly at aristocratic level, if for no other reason than that influential socialites who had backed the wrong horse in supporting the ex-King could threaten the unstable position of the new sovereigns – and this in spite of a national Press predominantly favourable to them. And in the course of that consolidation the Duchess of York, now Queen Elizabeth, came in for a great deal of criticism, primarily at the hands of those who were convinced that her brother-in-law had had a bad deal.

Ten days after the abdication Perry Brownlow, King Edward's close friend who had been instrumental in facilitating many of the journeys and meetings between him and Mrs Simpson, was summarily sacked as the

North London to North Island, New Zealand. (Below) the Queen Mother as Patron of the London Gardens Scheme, visited an infants' school at Queen's Crescent, St Pancras in June 1957. Three days later she accompanied her brother-in-law the Duke of Gloucester (right) to France for the unveiling of the Dunkirk Memorial to 4,700 troops of the British Expeditionary Force who died without known graves in Belgium and France. The following month the Queen Mother visited Northern Rhodesia, attending a garden party at Government House, Lusaka (left) on 13th July. In October, having been appointed Counsellor of State during her daughter's absence abroad, she took Princess Anne to Heathrow Airport (opposite page, bottom right) to await the return of the Queen and Prince Philip from their State Visit to the United States. In 1958, the Queen Mother toured New Zealand, visiting the Karitane Hospital, near Wellington, of which she laid the foundation stone 31 years earlier, and which she visited again (below right) during her last visit in 1966.

King's Lord-in-Waiting and the news outraged the ex-King's friends who alleged small-mindedness, feared the beginnings of a purge, and suspected the new Queen of wielding a power which the King was thought to be too gentle to exercise himself. Even Chips Channon who had long since resigned himself to being "out of the royal racket" was indignant though, knowing the Queen of old, guessed her to be free from blame: "I cannot believe that it is Queen Elizabeth's doing," he wrote. "She is not so foolish. It is those old courtiers . . ." Nevertheless it could not be said that the Queen was particularly keen to tolerate reminders of the previous reign, and certainly she was determined not to allow the present reign to be blighted by a rump reaction. Like Queen Mary, and not without justification, she feared that the fairly amicable basis on which the two brothers had parted would lead to unwelcome, if

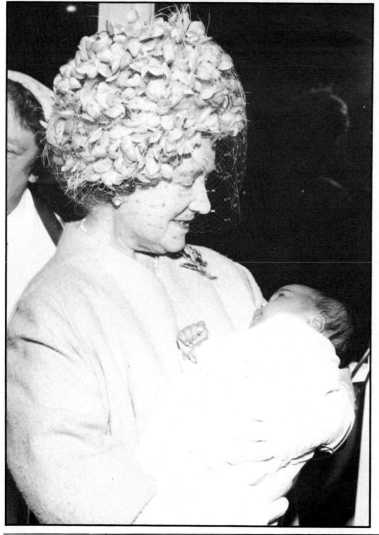

Visiting New Zealand early in 1958, the Queen Mother became the first member of the Royal Family to fly round the world. She was in splendid form, as (opposite page, far left) at Christchurch in February. Owing to successive failures in the American aircraft which had taken her from place to place on the tour (left) her return home was delayed, and she travelled the last leg by Britannia airline, arriving back (below far right) in mid-March to be greeted by the Queen, Princess Anne and Princess Margaret. At her "welcome home" reception at the Guildhall (right) she referred to the delays in a witty reference to Devon Loch's collapse at the 1956 Grand National. "I have some experience of the disappointment of seeing a dazzling success snatched from one, even after the last fence, and my sympathy is . . . with the gallant crews who worked so unceasingly . . ." (Opposite page, centre right) the Queen Mother at the dedication service at St Clement Danes, in October 1958. Two weeks later at St Margaret's Westminster (opposite page, bottom right). Her Chancellorship of London University began in 1955 and she attended almost every Foundation Day award ceremony (below right, in November 1958) until her resignation in 1980.

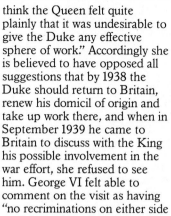

think the Queen felt quite plainly that it was undesirable to give the Duke any effective sphere of work." Accordingly she is believed to have opposed all suggestions that by 1938 the Duke should return to Britain, renew his domicil of origin and take up work there, and when in September 1939 he came to Britain to discuss with the King his possible involvement in the war effort, she refused to see him. George VI felt able to comment on the visit as having "no recriminations on either side . . . I found him the same as I had always known him," but the Duke went away empty-handed. He received nothing more challenging than a posting to the Bahamas where he was Governor-General for five years, and the then Colonial Secretary Lord Lloyd is on record as opining that it was the King's own idea to keep the Windsors out of England. That perennial nettle, the question of the Duchess receiving the title of Royal Highness, was never grasped and the Duke abandoned his crusade after his recommendation for such a grant as part of the 1943 New

well-meant, attempts by the ex-King to influence the new one, and the Duke of Windsor's frequent telephone calls to his brother in the early months of the reign overflowed with constitutional, political and procedural advice. Those conversations were soon halted – at whose instance we are not entirely certain – but the wider question of giving the Duke of Windsor some useful work to perform on behalf of the King in a private capacity was steadfastly resisted by the Queen, for reasons which that talented go-between during the Abdication crisis, Walter Monckton, fully appreciated. It was his opinion that the Queen "naturally thought that she must be on her guard because the Duke of Windsor, to whom the other brothers had always looked up, was an attractive, vital creature who might be a rallying-point for many who might be more critical of the new King who was less superficially endowed with the arts and graces that please. I

Year Honours, to recognise the Duchess' war work, was turned down by the King who, it seems, had no appetite for declaring the truth outright to his frustrated, if obstinate, brother.

Whatever the King's feelings on the subject, and the evidence points to a bitter regret at the inextricable twists of successive events, the Queen's resolve remained constant and far-sighted. From the beginning of their reign she fully realised the paramount importance of seeing her reluctant but dutiful husband established not just constitutionally but also in hearts and minds as the rightful King, and she looked forward with great single-mindedness to the immediate future, echoing Queen Mary's insistence that he needed sympathy and support. She was livid when, shortly after the Duke of Windsor's marriage in June 1937 someone reported to her that the Duchess had done wonders for him and commented that he had stopped drinking and had no unsightly pouches beneath his eyes. "Yes," she replied: "Who has the lines under his eyes now?" Indeed she found it difficult to forget that all the strains, both mental and

was concerned. Conscious of the fury of Queen Mary and the other Royal ladies she felt secure in adopting an uncompromising stance in refusing to receive her, and indeed grudging the remotest acknowledgement of her. In pursuit of this rigid attitude, comprehensible perhaps only in yesterday's context, she was prepared to withstand the reported abuses heaped upon her by both the Duke and the Duchess of Windsor. Queen Mary's pivotal role was allegedly mocked by the Duchess who described the reign of George VI as a "split-level matriarchy in pants. Queen Mary runs the King's wife and the wife runs the King." Chips Channon plaintively noted in 1937 that "certainly she (Queen Mary) and the Court hate Wallis Simpson to the point of hysteria . . . They would be better advised to be civil if it is beyond their courage to be cordial!" But by and large it never happened. The Gloucesters and the Mountbattens kept in occasional touch, and Queen Mary once sent "a kind message to your wife" in a letter to her "poor, silly son." But at the end of the Second World War, the

physical imposed upon her husband had been caused by what Queen Mary persisted in describing as King Edward's "dereliction of duty." If she resented the possibility of her husband being upstaged by his predecessor, she was adamant where the Duchess of Windsor

In April 1959 the Queen Mother and Princess Margaret toured Italy: (top) attending a reception at the British Embassy in Rome. They visited Tivoli (right) before returning home via Paris where they lunched with President de Gaulle at the Elysée Palace (above).

funeral of the Princess Royal in 1965, and again the following year when the Duke came to London for an eye operation. When, in June 1967, a fortnight after the centenary of her birth, a plaque to the memory of Queen Mary was unveiled in the wall of Marlborough House, the Duchess was at last seen in the ranks of the Royal Family, exchanging a few quick words with her sister-in-law the Queen Mother, though not curtseying to her as she did to the Queen. That was the only public encounter between the two old adversaries until the Duke's own funeral in June 1972 when the Duchess, under intolerable

(Below) the Queen Mother arriving at, and (below left) leaving the Vatican where she and Princess Margaret met Pope John XXIII. That evening they attended a reception given by President Gronchi (top left) at the Quirinal. (Left) visiting the Villa d'Este, Tivoli.

Duke came to Windsor alone, as he did for the funerals of King George in 1952 and Queen Mary in 1953. Several private visits passed unnoticed, and recognition for the Duchess remained wanting when the family gathered again for the

stress and heavily sedated, may just have been conscious of the clasp of hands and the Queen Mother's murmured condolences.

Considering the immediate aftermath of the Abdication it would be almost facile to state that the new Queen harboured no illusions about the task that lay ahead. Melbourne may have admired the quiet courage of the eighteen-year-old Queen Victoria as she assumed a discredited Throne, and Churchill was later to romanticise the vision of a young charming Queen following her well-loved father in 1952, but the maturer years of the King and Queen in December 1936 were no bar to public admiration. The archangel who would, according to Macaulay, have shrunk from the prospect of Victoria's destiny in 1837 would have viewed the implications of the unexpected accession almost a century later with equal or greater distaste. The speed of the events leading up to the Abdication caught the Press napping when the crisis

was resolved, but there was no doubt that every stop was pulled out to launch King George and Queen Elizabeth into their reign. A mass of articles and editorials praised them to the skies, hailing them as thoroughly worthy of the monarchy's fine traditions and crediting them with all the qualities and advantages they had attributed to King Edward VIII only eleven months before. The *Daily Sketch* was not alone in describing the new King as approximating most, of all the royal sons, to his father's kingly conception of national duty. "He and his Queen," it went on, "have continued to uphold in the noblest fashion the family traditions which have been the cornerstone of our social life and the sure guard of the Monarchy's prestige." This vaporous commendation seems

in perspective perversely sycophantic, but in spite of the elder brother's unquestioned charm, good looks and (as it was then thought) competence, there was and is nothing so appealing as a monarch with a family – King Edward himself had praised it as a "matchless blessing" in his parting speech, and the Abdication provided Britain and its Empire with precisely that emotional benefit. Beyond that and the plaudits of the nation as epitomised by the enormous crowd that waited to cheer the new King back to his home in Piccadilly on 11th December the Queen, to whom the more active, positive role appears to have fallen, must have perceived signs of a favourable start. The King's characteristic reticence was a definite disadvantage, his halting speech and severe looks compared badly with his predecessor's smooth confidence. The recent crises had quite unnerved him and he did not survive its stresses without breaking down and sobbing "like a child" in the presence of his mother. Though

he possessed an inner strength which had already seen him surmount several difficulties and would see him through more, he seemed to require constant encouragement and reassurance that his sense of dedication to an unenviable job was bearing fruit. Naturally it was his wife to whom he turned for this and, by far the more confident of the two – photographs which appear to illustrate this abound – she was able to provide it.

She did so predominantly by example. Encouraged by Queen Mary's considerate plea in her own recent address to the nation – "... I commend my dear daughter-in-law ... May she receive the same unfailing affection and trust which you have given to me for six and twenty years" – she set about making her role as Queen

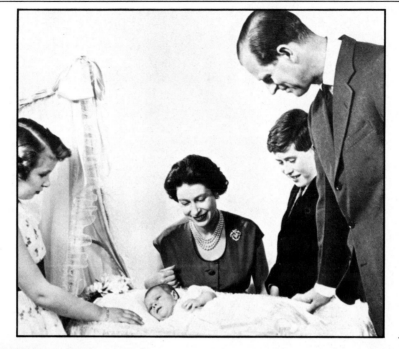

Consort as positive and definitive a statement of dedication as had Queen Mary – though liberally seasoned with enjoyment. It took time, of course. In March 1937 Harold Nicolson noticed how, at a royal dinner party the Queen "did the rounds, wearing upon her face a faint smile indicative of how she would have liked her dinner party were it not for the fact that she was Queen of England." This hesitancy was probably due to what she called the "intolerable honour" when she confided her impressions to another politician, Duff Cooper, the following month. But by the time of the Coronation in May 1937 the Queen was well settled in. She could have had little doubt of her popularity: her features were already adorning thousands of Coronation

Prince Andrew's birth in February 1960 gave the Queen Mother her first grandchild for almost ten years. On her 60th birthday the following August Prince Charles and Princess Anne took him to see her at Clarence House (opposite page and above). Cecil Beaton provided a portfolio of official pictures of the Queen and her third child (right) and of the entire family (top), which were issued to coincide with Prince Andrew's christening in March.

souvenirs from the noblest likenesses on statuettes to the unflattering printed portraits on handkerchiefs and ungainly plaster busts, and few households in the Kingdom spent the year unadorned by one or other well-loved souvenir of its supreme national event. Late in April she attended the F.A. Cup Final and presented the cup to Sunderland amid frenzied cheering far beyond the normal perfunctory respect afforded by football fans towards the Royal Family.

Once the ordeal of the Coronation was over there was no stopping her, and through her the King gained in stature too. Ramsay McDonald told the Queen in May 1937 that "the King had come on magnificently since his accession." Gratified at this she asked, "Am I doing all right?" to which the old Red renegade made a sweeping gesture with his arms and said "Oh, you . . ." as if the answer were more than obvious. Chips

(Left) the Queen Mother leaves Clarence House shortly after Viscount Linley's birth, 3rd November 1961, to visit the Royal Holloway College, and a week later plants her cross in the Field of Remembrance, St Margaret's Westminster (opposite page, top left). In May 1962 she met 92-year-old Sister Margaret Meredith, holder of the Eastern Star, at a Boer War veterans' service at Chelsea (opposite page, top right). In September (far left) she visited Perth to celebrate her 25th anniversary as Colonel-in-Chief of the Black Watch Regiment.

Channon charted the royal progress in the early years of the reign. He admitted that the King and Queen were "popular – very – and increasingly so," but, no doubt still smarting from the consequences of his friend's abdication complained that "they have no message for the Labour party who believe them, and rightly I fear, to be the puppets of a Palace clique. Certainly they are too hemmed in by the territorial aristocracy and have all the faults which Edward VIII lacked in this particular field." This was a strange element of the royal character for Channon of all people to score on and condemn but his pique was soon outrun by his admiration. At a ball given by the Duke and Duchess of Sutherland in May 1937 he "noticed how both the King and the Queen have gained in presence and in dignity." Five months later he attended the first State Opening of Parliament of the reign and found that "the King seemed quite at ease, and so did the Queen." By this time Harold Nicolson, no great supporter of the ex-King, was convinced that the new King and Queen were right for the job. He had in particular met the Queen at the dinner party two months before the Coronation and was bowled over by "the charm and dignity which she displays. I cannot help feeling what a mess poor Mrs Simpson would have made of such an occasion. It demonstrated to us more than anything else how wholly impossible that marriage would have been."

Quite clearly she had risen magnificently to her unexpected new role in much the same way as she had assimilated the royal lifestyle on becoming Duchess of York in 1923. She now, of course, had the additional responsibility of making the change in circumstance palatable to her two growing children to whom Buckingham Palace was familiar only in part. The Yorks as a family had never lived there and the children had rarely been other than casual visitors to its private apartments. Now with the Palace empty of occupants – Queen Mary had moved across to Marlborough House shortly before the Abdication – the sudden change of surroundings allowed the Royal Family no latitude for preparation or adjustment, as the fifth monarch to do so took up official residence. To the Queen fell the tasks, which might have been pleasant in more leisurely circumstances, of making homely the royal apartments which Queen Mary had emptied of her many hundreds of personal treasures, of supervising the removal and

repositioning of the family possessions which had accumulated at 145 Piccadilly, and of helping to design a system of private apartments – uncalled for since Queen Victoria's day – in which the princesses' accommodation was sufficiently close to their parents' suites for the family unit to flourish.

In addition, since in deference to the notions of continuity and good order, the original date for the Coronation as fixed by King Edward VIII – 12th May 1937 – was not altered by his successor,

(Right) another more formal 63rd birthday portrait of the Queen Mother, taken by Anthony Buckley. (Below) deputising for the Queen, who had recently left for her second visit to Australia, the Queen Mother arrives at Buckingham Palace to carry out an Investiture in February 1963. (Below left) still smiling, she accompanies Princess Margaret in a closed carriage on a rainy second day at Royal Ascot that June. (Left) attending the Royal Variety Performance with the Snowdons in November 1963.

the new Queen was inescapably and fully involved for five hectic months in plans for this supreme event. Basic plans were already well advanced of course, but revised procedures to accommodate the crowning of the consort as well as the King, provision for her attendants, allowances for new invitees, and for original invitees who might no longer wish to attend, progressively complex planning committee considerations, and host of minor and more personal decisions had now to be embraced. As on previous royal occasions, these included the knotty question of the role of the broadcasting media which again became the subject of hot and formidable debate. Ultimately it was agreed that a further innovation should be permitted – that of having the Coronation service filmed and broadcast live, but with television cameras (then a

complete novelty) restricted to outside coverage only. At the other end of the decision-making process the Queen decided to wear the famous Koh-I-Noor diamond as the principal jewel in her crown. The diamond, which was presented to Queen Victoria in 1850 is thought to bring ill-luck on any man who wears it, but Queen Elizabeth was content to rely on its history as the bringer of good fortune to its female wearers. The dictates of superstition may well have been made more easy by what many contemporary observers saw as the patent and solemn attitude of faith with which both the King and Queen approached their Coronation. In today's sceptical world it is

(Top right) the Queen Mother visiting the London Gardens Scheme prize-winner in Hackney in July 1955. (Above right) attending a gala performance of Tosca at Covent Garden in July 1965. Her 1964 visit to Australia and New Zealand had to be postponed owing to an emergency operation for appendicitis. She had met the Australian High Commissioner in London at the end of January (top left) before the proposed tour, but was whisked into King Edward VII Hospital for Officers four days later. She was discharged, fully recovered, on 16th February (opposite page, top left) and the Australian visit took place in 1966. (Opposite page, bottom left) inspecting a guard of honour on arrival at Bluff, New Zealand, on the southernmost tip of South Island, and (opposite page, right) attending a concert in Wellington. Meeting the Maoris was, of course, inevitable (above).

soon after the Abdication a letter of genuine appreciation to him which she signed "Yours for the first time and with great affection, Elizabeth R." In it she revealed with quiet satisfaction that "I can hardly now believe that we have been called to this tremendous task and the curious thing is that we are not afraid. I feel that God has enabled us to face the situation calmly." Now, not long after an incident in which she is reputed to have lost her nerve and cried out, "I can't go through with it! I can't be

observed from the attitude and behaviour of the King and Queen that there was "no doubt they had entered on this task with a real religious sense." The Coronation festivities began well enough – from the sumptuous State Banquet for 450 people in the Ball and Supper Room at Buckingham Palace to the moving personal interludes in which the King complimented his wife's indispensable support by offering her the South African-jewelled insignia of the Thistle –

almost fashionable to wonder about the sincerity of any public act of worship in the course of a function of State, but in 1937, far from emulating the sort of public behaviour which had caused Bishop Blunt of Bradford to speak out so uncompromisingly against Edward VIII,

the King and Queen made no secret of their religious faith. The Bishop of St Alban's felt able to write to the Queen pointing out the religious significance of the forthcoming Coronation while the Queen, already a good friend of the Archbishop of Canterbury, wrote

crowned!" she and her husband met the Archbishop on the Sunday before the Coronation for a discussion about the spiritual meaning of the rite. "I gave them my personal blessing," noted the Archbishop afterwards. "There were tears in their eyes when we rose from our knees. From that moment I knew what would be in their hearts when they came to their anointing and crowning." The Poet Laureate, John Masefield echoed the sentiment in his "Prayer for the King's Reign":–
"Grant to our Queen the strength that lifts and shares
The daily burden that a monarch bears,"
and some weeks after the Coronation Harold Nicolson

thus making her the first ever Lady of that great Scottish Order – and in which Queen Mary presented her daughter-in-law with a tortoiseshell and diamond fan which had once belonged to Queen Alexandra. The King received from her a dark blue enamel snuffbox bearing miniatures of his parents. But Coronation Day itself – like the Wedding Day in 1923 – proved to be dull and showery and the Queen's procession to Westminster Abbey was halted when a chaplain fainted *en route* and could not conveniently be removed to receive first aid. The ceremony itself was full of mistakes and near misses, all of which were duly noted by the King, who later confessed to

Ramsay MacDonald that for long periods during the ceremony he was unaware of what he was doing.

Unusually for her, Queen Mary, whose sense of occasion led her to break with the tradition whereby the widow of a previous sovereign did not attend the Coronation of any successor, was unaware of any mistakes. "Bertie and Elizabeth looked so well when they came in and did it all beautifully," she recorded, thrilled on the verge of her seventieth birthday to have witnessed the crowning of the first consort since the sixteenth century to come of British stock. The irrepressible Chips Channon soaked up the scene as

(Below) a day's relaxation for the Queen Mother in New Zealand: fishing for trout on the Clutha River near Lake Wanaka in April 1966. She was home again to parades at Chelsea: (right) her first visit to the Founder's Day Parade at Royal Hospital in June and (below right) with members of the South African War Veterans' Association at Chelsea Barracks in July. (Below left) visiting the Commonwealth cemetery at Bocklingen during a three-day visit to Germany in 1965. (Left) the Queen, Prince Philip and their sons leaving Liverpool Street Station en route from Sandringham to Buckingham Palace in January 1966. Prince Edward was then almost two years old.

that Consort entered the Abbey wearing her dress of ivory satin and a magnificent purple velvet robe and train, embroidered with the emblems of the principal Dominions of the Empire and carried by six trainbearers. "She appeared dignified but smiling," he commented, adding – with a touch of mischief perhaps triggered off by persistent rumours that the Queen was pregnant – "and much more bosomy." Princesses Elizabeth and Margaret attended as well; supervised by Queen Mary they witnessed the solemn and unforgettable moment of their mother's consecration as the Archbishop blessed her, anointed her as she sat concealed beneath a canopy of cloth of gold held by four duchesses, and finally placed the consort's crown, set into Queen Victoria's circlet, upon her head. Who would have noticed the irony as, following this sacred procedure, the King's right-hand woman took her place on his left-hand side?

Perhaps it was the suddenness of the Queen's emergence as the commanding social personality of the day; perhaps it was her eventual unashamed enjoyment of the role she was at such short notice called upon to play. Whatever the reason, it is inescapable that the years between the Accession in 1936 and the outbreak of war three years later seemed to mark a peak of feminine fulfilment for her. Harold Nicolson has already

(Below) the Queen Mother meets Sea Scouts at Bluff, during her 1966 New Zealand visit. (Right) she attends St Paul's Cathedral in April 1969 for President Eisenhower's memorial service; (opposite page, bottom) leaving with Prince Philip afterwards. (Opposite page, top) arriving with the Queen at Westminster Abbey for a service in memory of Princess Marina, October 1968. (Bottom picture) the Queen Mother with Lord Mountbatten and King Carl XVI of Sweden at Holyroodhouse in 1975, during his State Visit to Britain.

testified to the ease with which she assumed her role as Queen Consort – as easily in fact as she had made the transition from commoner to royal in 1923 – and it seemed to contemporary observers that she was not afraid to advertise the fact by her delectable behaviour on occasions both formal and informal, and by her distinctly heightened sense of fashion. Her features, though much beloved and greatly envied, never aspired to the classically beautiful – an attribute which by the 1930s had in any case come to connote coldness and lack of recognisable human character. She always had the looks which one might patronisingly describe as "bonny" in girlhood, and essentially warm and kind as a young woman. The smile which might have made her famous even had she not been royal, developed from a combination of the gentlest movement of the lips as evidenced in many early portraits, and the almost cheeky grin of sheer enjoyment which accompanied her various social exploits.

Though her status as a Royal Duchess, and ultimately as Queen, were bound to evince compliments upon her appearance, her attractive, smooth, pale skin, cornflower blue eyes and soft, dark hair fringed from early womanhood until shortly after the Coronation, were for years the talk of the town. "I have never seen a clearer complexion or a sweeter or more steadfast expression," wrote the *Daily Sketch's* gossip columnist on the day of her husband's Accession. "Though short, she has the dignity of a *grande dame.*" Even the Duchess of Windsor, after one of their earliest meetings at Fort Belvedere, wrote later of "her justly famed charm" and was "also aware of the beauty of her complexion and the almost startling blueness of her eyes." While Sir Gerald Kelly, who painted the official State portraits of the King and Queen in 1938, praised "the admiration and affection which grew all round her. From wherever one looked at her she looked nice: her face, her smile, her skin, her colouring – everything was right."

Like any woman conscious of her good looks, she complemented them with the very best in clothes. She had been as ready as any to adopt the exciting new fashion of the

immediate post-war years, though she never made the mistake of becoming an eccentric dresser, as many contemporaries did. She was, one observer gratefully noted, "the quiet sort, not one of those ultra-modern types," and she was content to let the long and ever more daring crazes of the flappers pass her by. At the time of her wedding, the conservative quality newspapers were relieved, if not positively thrilled, by her lack of "modernity" (a word which in those days connoted extremism) and lauded her clear aversion to the "flat boyish outline so much admired today." In spite of King George V's antipathy to them – he never allowed Queen Mary to wear one – she popularised those famous cloche hats – "Did we really use to wear those funny hats?" she was to say half a century later – and the wrap-over coat which finds a parallel in many of her light summery coats today were even then very much in favour with her. Fundamentally, whether she was wearing "the lightest and flimsiest material" – the description accorded to her honeymoon trousseau – or was swamped by the heavy, unflattering Bardic robes which she was obliged to wear at the Eisteddfodd at Swansea in 1926, she was invariably – to use a word which her sister-in-law the Duchess of Kent disapproved – smart.

In the 1930s the fashionable requirement changed considerably. The close-fitting hats gave way to large, fanciful picture hats with enormous brims. Long, floaty dresses superseded the short, straight skirts of the previous decade, and parasols, with which Queen Mary herself had never dispensed, came back into fashion. The new luxuriant look reached its peak in the years immediately before the Second World War, when Norman Hartnell, one of whose earliest royal assignments had been to design a wedding dress for the Duchess of Gloucester in 1935, was snapped up by the Duchess of York. When she became Queen he effectively became Couturier Royal, and no royal patronage could have been better timed. His first years in his enviable new station

The Investiture of Prince Charles as Prince of Wales in 1969 sparked off great renewed interest in the Royal Family after four or five leanish years – the more so because of the growing number of royal children. The Queen Mother's own children and grandchildren, seen (left) after Morning Service at Sandringham in January 1969, were well enough known, but a photograph taken outside St George's Chapel, Windsor on Christmas Day 1969 (opposite page, bottom) shows the increasing contingent of cousins, with James and Marina Ogilvy, children of Princess Alexandra, flanking the group, and George, Earl of St Andrews and Lady Helen Windsor, the Kent children, in the middle along with Prince Andrew, Prince Edward, Viscount Linley and (second from left) Lady Sarah Armstrong-Jones. (Right) the Queen Mother's 70th birthday portrait, by Cecil Beaton. She was still as active as ever: in March 1969 she honoured, as usual, the Irish Guards by presenting shamrocks at Victoria Barracks, Windsor and gave special attention to their mascot, the Irish wolfhound Fionn (below). In June

1970 she attended a service in Westminster Abbey commemorating the centenary of Charles Dickens' death: (bottom right) with the Dean of Westminster after the service.

coincided with the pre-war heyday of European fashion houses, and the Queen was the willing beneficiary of all their influence on his efforts to lend flair to the current expression of royalty as a social and diplomatic force.

That attitude was particularly relevant for the State Visit to France, which the King and Queen undertook as the first of their reign in 1938. The visit had been scheduled to begin on 28th June, the one hundredth anniversary of Queen Victoria's Coronation, but the death, five days before, of the Countess of Strathmore threw the arrangements into confusion. The Queen, saddened at this unfortunate coincidence as much by the loss of a dearly-loved mother, went immediately into deep mourning, and the journey to France was

subsequently postponed until 19th July. It was almost delayed again by the King's severe attack of gastric influenza, but that passed in time for the visit to begin as freshly arranged. The Queen left Britain still dressed in black, but her arrival in France could not have been more surprising. Using the widespread European practice of wearing white for mourning as a convenient excuse, she stepped onto French soil, confident and smiling in brilliant white, and the entire three-day visit was carried out in the same elegant vein. Extravagantly sweeping Edwardian-style gowns predominated, along with crinolines said to have been inspired by Winterhalter's famous portraits of the young Queen Victoria, all complementing the fine, favourable summer weather and the theatrical outdoor performances of song and dance which the French put on for their royal guests. The Queen's graceful, airy wardrobe was perfectly shown off by her slow, dignified gait – what Chips

press. "We have taken the Queen to our hearts. She rules over two nations."

The visit was of course a declaration of solidarity in the face of what many people saw as a coming conflict with Germany, and the following months were heavy with diplomatic activity all over Western Europe, devoted to staving off what ultimately proved unstoppable. Much of Mr Chamberlain's business as Prime Minister necessitated the King's continued presence in London, and he was unable to be present for the grand launching of the liner *Queen Elizabeth* at the end of September 1938. The Queen travelled to Clydeside alone, passing on her husband's words of comfort in phrases now famous for their rather quaint, old fashioned optimism: "I have a message for you from the King. He bids the people of this country to be of good cheer..." But cheer was hard to come by in those lowering days of continued political crises. Even when, in May 1939, the King and Queen sailed to the New

Channon later called "her curious sideways lilting walk" – and balanced by her sizeable collection of huge, frilled, wide-brimmed hats and delicate white lace parasols. The French, impressed as much by this vision as by her competent, easy command of their language, were immediately won over. "Today France is a monarchy again," trumpeted the Parisian

A second set of Cecil Beaton studies marked the Queen Mother's 70th birthday, an anniversary widely trumpeted by generous press tributes. These (top and opposite page) were taken at Royal Lodge, Windsor, against a typical and appropriate backdrop of rhododendrons. (Above and right) attending the Sovereign's Parade at Sandhurst in April 1972.

World, they had to forego the originally planned use of the battleship *Repulse,* in case it was required at short notice for war service: they travelled in the liner *Empress of Australia* instead. For the Queen in particular, the trip was greatly exciting, and the adrenalin certainly flowed when she found that the ship was surrounded by icebergs off the coast of Newfoundland. "We very nearly hit an iceberg the day before yesterday," she wrote to Queen Mary, "and the poor Captain was nearly demented because some kind cheerful people kept reminding him that it was about here that the *Titanic* was struck and just about the same date."

The drifting ice floes held them up, they berthed safely on 17th May at Quebec, and King George became the first British reigning sovereign to tread on the soil of what was then fondly known as British North America. The tour was a resounding success. Travel was mostly by the "silver and blue train" as it was familiarly known – a three hundred-ton blue and aluminium CPR locomotive pulling twelve streamlined coaches over a total of more than 9,000 miles in the course of the six-week tour from Quebec to Vancouver and back to Halifax. At every station – and with a programme which left very little time for relaxation there were many stations – there was a crowd to greet the King and Queen. For their part, they had given instructions to be alerted whenever well-wishers were spotted by the side of the railway line, so that their long wait could be properly rewarded.

Like most tours, this one had its formal and informal moments. For the Queen, the laying of the foundation stone for the new Supreme Court building in Ottawa was perhaps the most memorable. She mused on the fact that she, and not the King, had been asked to lay the stone, but concluded that the choice was appropriate as "woman's position in modern society has depended upon the growth of law." Among the more informal interludes was the private visit to see the famous Dionne quins who had been born in Canada six years earlier. The Queen herself was credited with almost

In March 1972 the Queen Mother was at Pirbright, again presenting shamrocks to the Irish Guards. She met a veteran guardsman (left) who was awarded the VC in 1917. Two months later the Duke of Windsor died after a long illness from cancer. This brought his Duchess to England by royal invitation for the first time since 1967 when, with the Duke, she landed at Southampton (opposite page, below left) to attend the unveiling of a memorial plaque to Queen Mary at Marlborough House. The ex-King's funeral took place at Windsor in June 1972, though his widow – seen (opposite page) with the Queen, Prince Philip and the Queen Mother, was heavily sedated at the time and is unlikely to remember much of it. (Below) the Queen Mother with Prince William of Gloucester at his brother's wedding at Barnwell in July 1972. Six weeks later he too was dead, killed at the age of 30 in an air crash.

miraculous powers when, despite persistent rain during a drive through Winnipeg, she instructed that the car's roof should be let down so that people could see her. Almost immediately the rain stopped! But she seemed to have enough personal magic of her own. As one commentator said: "As for the Queen she appeared and the day was won. So simple in her bearing and yet so refined, so spontaneous in every movement and yet so harmonious, so radiant with feminine charm and so expressive of emotion, she also found the true words for every occasion and every person." Lord Tweedsmuir, Canada's Governor General, praised the Queen's creditable acquittal of her duties with the grateful sincerity of one for whom the organisation of such a massive enterprise proved well worth the effort. "The Queen has a perfect genius for the right

kind of publicity. The unrehearsed episodes were marvellous," he wrote, and went on to describe how popular she had been for ignoring the set programme and wandering towards the crowds to meet them personally. The Queen enjoyed the tour too: "It made us," she confided to the Canadian Prime Minister, Mr. Mackenzie King, and she was no doubt pleased that her impeccable French had once again stood her in good stead with the French-speaking communities in the east of the country.

The tour was almost as famous for the few days the King and Queen spent in the United States, where they were the guests of President Franklin D. Roosevelt and his accomplished wife Eleanor. It was Mrs. Roosevelt, in fact, who arranged with the Queen for one little girl, young Diana Hopkins, the

daughter of F.D.R.'s personal assistant, to meet her. The young lady, Mrs. Roosevelt warned, had envisaged the Queen wearing crown and sceptre so, in order not to disappoint her, the Queen considerately decided that the meeting had better take place when she was fully dressed in tiara and jewels, ready for a formal dinner. The President's informal style was much appreciated by his guest, the modest retiring King, and their personal letters to each other – "My dear President Roosevelt," "My dear King George" – reflected the kindred spirits. Perhaps the most informal incident of the trip came when, after a private evening dinner and a long talk, the President suddenly turned to the King and paternalistically told him, "Well, young man, it's time for you to go to bed!"

Apart from the great personal success the King and Queen scored with the President, the triumphant reception accorded to them by the people of New York and the Atlantic sea-board surpassed all precedents. Shouts of "Attaboy, Queen" followed in their wake and one admiring Senator told King George, "My, you're a great Queen-picker!" When, to protect herself from the blazing sunshine in Washington, the Queen first put up a parasol – in pure white silk

(Far right) the Queen Mother, at the London Palladium for 1970's Royal Variety Performance, receives a bouquet from five-year-old Steven Winson. (Below) meeting the owners of the Heim Gallery in Jermyn Street at the opening of an exhibition of Italian baroque art in May 1973. (Opposite page, below)

with some of the 500 standard-bearers at the dedication of the new British Legion Women's Section Standard at Westminster Abbey in March 1974. (Top left) on the narrow boat Jubilee after opening a newly dredged 17-mile stretch of Avon waterway in June 1974. (Right) arriving at London's Guildhall for a reception in October 1974 marking the 50th anniversary of the Royal Auxiliary Air Force. (Centre right) greeted by Prince Charles on arrival at London University in November 1975 for an awards presentation which included his own honorary degree of Doctor of Laws. (Top) another visit to the Field of Remembrance – in November 1979.

with dark green lining – the parasol became an instant and indispensable part of the East Coast fashionable scene. "To makers of parasols and umbrellas," asserted *Life* magazine, "the reign of George and Elizabeth will ever be the period when a Queen and a Prime Minister raised the parasol and the umbrella to unprecedented pinnacles of international significance and chic." It was, unwittingly a grim reminder of the state to which international affairs had been brought after the humiliation of Munich, and another one became apparent when the Italian press, the

mouth-piece of Mussolini, made great and hypocritical play of the fact that Mrs. Roosevelt failed to curtsey to Queen Elizabeth on greeting her: incredibly they called it the greatest scandal of the present era.
But these were insignificant elements in a tour of sublime popularity and triumph for the King and Queen. An American newspaper article voted the Queen "Woman of the Year" because "arriving in an aloof and critical country, she completely conquered it and accomplished the conquest by being her natural self." As for the King, everybody wondered how on earth such a "nice guy" could

possibly be a descendant of George III. But George III's descendant and his wife had without doubt overwhelmed the old Colonies at their first attempt. Nevertheless, the hard realities of life were not lost on Mrs. Roosevelt as she and the President joined the crowds in an emotional rendering of Auld Lang Syne as the Royal Train pulled out of Hyde Park Station at the end of the Washington visit. "We all knew," she wrote "that the King and Queen were returning home to face a war." It was strange how history was repeating itself. That last, brilliant spring and summer of 1939, so much enjoyed by the King and Queen in North America, was eerily so comparable to the sumer of 1914

just before the curtain closed on the finery and grandeur of a golden age. The last of Hitler's pushes – the invasion of Poland – was as widely and fully expected for well over a month as was the Kaiser's entry into the Balkan conflict of June 1914, yet, as in 1914, the logical prospect of war was everywhere avoided as unthinkable. Queen Mary, who a quarter of a century before had been Queen Consort for almost as short a time as Queen Elizabeth was now, wrote to her daughter-in-law in those last days of constant anxiety, her solace mingled with her unfailing sense of history: "I feel deeply for you, too, I having gone through all this in August 1914 when I was the wife of the Sovereign."

When war finally came, at 11 o'clock on Sunday 3rd September, the Queen was still at Balmoral with the two Princesses. She came down South to join the King immediately, leaving her daughters to complete as much as possible of what would be their last proper summer holiday at Queen Victoria's famous Highland retreat. For Balmoral became one of the Royal Family's war casualties, being closed down for the six-year duration of hostilities. Sandringham was another victim: shortly after Christmas 1939 the Big House was closed and its lawns and golf course ploughed up for food production, though in 1943 the King and his family would spend a short harvest-time holiday on the estate. Windsor Castle was a sorry sight compared with its peacetime glories – all pictures and hangings were removed and boxed, furniture was put into safe storage and its many resounding corridors were only

Popular belief names Prince Charles as the Queen Mother's favourite grandson, on the strength of pictures like Peter Sellers' portrait (top) at Royal Lodge for her 75th birthday, or of the Prince escorting his grandmother at Ascot in 1978 (right), or at this dedication service at St Paul's in November 1979 (left). As President of the Royal College of Music, the Queen Mother is an annual visitor; (above) in November 1977 and (opposite page, top) in November 1979. (Far left) another of her many attendances at St Paul's Cathedral, in 1978.

dimly lit by single electric lights. And Buckingham Palace itself, grand and solid as it was, did not escape the immediate effect of the austerities of war. Even its most august wartime guest, Mrs Eleanor Roosevelt, had to suffer them: the Queen offered the use of her own bedroom which the President's wife was astounded to find both cold and damp – "just one little bar of electric fire

More foreign connections as, (below) the Queen Mother opened a British Culture Centre in Paris during a four-day visit in 1976, and (bottom picture) accompanied the Empress of Persia back to Clarence House after a London concert that April. Family connections, too: (right) the Queen Mother unveiled a portrait of Princess Anne during a visit to HMS Dauntless in 1976.

in the room" – while the daily quota of bathwater was limited to a few inches, and the grandiose royal crockery bore very ordinary canteen food. The exact degree of royal privations during the war has never been authoritatively documented. There were occasional supplies of game from the Royal estates, for instance, and it is unlikely that the special regulations governing food rations for official purposes were not extended to the Royal Family. But there can be no doubt that the King and Queen in particular shared the dangers common to their subjects in London and indeed all of Britain's major cities and industrial centres. It is almost certain that plans were well laid to whisk them away to safety in the event of a German invasion – an organisation called the Coates mission had in fact been established to remove them to one of four country houses – and arrangements for an eventual escape to Canada to head a Government in exile have been profusely rumoured. But while Britain remained uninvaded, the Queen voiced

both her preference for remaining in London and her conception of duty to do so. These emerged during a conversation with Harold Nicolson in July 1940, when he shamefacedly confessed having felt homesick whilst abroad recently. "But that is all right," answered the Queen. "That's personal patriotism. I should die if I had to leave." Her sense of duty in particular was explained in an oft-quoted chain of irrefutable logic on the question of the evacuation of her two daughters, in which she is reputed to have said, "They cannot go without me. I cannot go without the King. The King will never leave." That, in fact, left her open to criticism in that while she was encouraging the mothers of London to allow their children to be evacuated to unknown destinations – "We know what it means to be parted from our children," she assured them in a message broadcast on Armistice Day, 1939 – she kept her own children with her in London. When, however, the Blitz began in earnest some ten months later, Princesses

Elizabeth and Margaret were sent to Windsor to continue their studies while London braced itself for the fury of Hitler's all-night bombing. From the German point of view the bombardment of September 1940 was disappointing and unsuccessful but it sent the Londoners, for whom this was the first real taste of modern warfare, reeling. Vast areas of the closely packed East End were destroyed and hundreds of civilian lives were lost as makeshift air-raid shelters proved ineffective against the might of the Luftwaffe in full cry. Both the King and Queen – the Queen was later to describe the Cockney as "a great fighter" – paid immediate and almost unscheduled visits to the devastated suburbs, unable to do more than comfort the bereaved, show concern for the homeless and encourage those working to mitigate suffering. These visits became almost daily events as the constant and intense German attack bit deeper into London's morale – so deep, in fact, that the Royal couple were actually booed on

Lord Snowdon, divorced from Princess Margaret in 1978, took the delightful portrait of the Queen with her first grandson Peter Phillips (top) in April that year at Windsor. (Above) the Queen Mother and her daughters at West Newton Women's Institute near Sandringham in 1977. (Left) remembering the fallen at Westminster in November 1974.

one East End visit in mid-September. This hostility was a manifestation of what many politicians already feared – the breaking of the country's spirit in the face of hopeless odds – and even Clement Davies considered that by continuing to hammer away at the densely populated and deprived East End the Führer could effectively have occasioned anarchy in

Britain and solved many of his own problems into the bargain. But Hitler made the mistake of spreading the bombardment to London's West End, thus subjecting the wealthy to dangers and deprivations similar to the capital's poorer citizens. Not unexpectedly, Buckingham Palace itself came in for several air attacks and it may have been with some relief that the Queen was consequently able to say, after the most severe damage had been done, "I'm glad we've been bombed. It makes me feel I can look the East End in the face."

If life thus became somewhat more comfortable psychologically, its physical comforts fast began to disappear. Although

The Queen Mother's 80th year – an apogee of public recognition. Besides the great national celebrations in July 1980 (left, below left and opposite page, bottom picture), London provided a Rose Walk in St James's Park in her honour (below) and there were special cheers for her at the Garter Ceremony at Windsor (below, far left) and at the Trooping (right).

the only part of the Palace to receive a direct hit during a total of nine raids on it was the chapel – bombed during Morning Service with the loss of a hundred lives and of almost every chattel save the massive Royal Family Bible – extensive areas of the grounds and courtyards were hit, and much of the Palace's structure was reduced to so much rubble by

the impact. The main drainage system was blown and the Queen particularly remembered that "a great column of water came into the air" as a bomb was dropped from a plane which had flown straight up the Mall and over the Palace. She also remembered that the resulting flooding brought the rats out into the garden, and that "everyone had

great fun pursuing them." Holes gaped in roofs and ceilings – the Queen's own apartments were damaged when a bomb dropped straight through them, without exploding, into the ground floor rooms below – and an ingenious network of baths and buckets cluttered many passages and corridors when the rain came through. A new swimming pool, built for the family only two

years earlier, was cratered out of all recognition and before long no window remained intact throughout the entire building of six hundred rooms. Quite apart from the damage wrought by successive explosions, the King and Queen were unnerved by the risks of unexploded bombs, one of which is even today thought to be embedded deep down "somewhere in the garden, I suppose," and by the fact that "one really wasn't quite sure what was going to disappear next."

They nevertheless decided that, in the Queen's words "we stay put with our people" and, despite the repeated strain of seeing, not only at first hand but also at first opportunity, when

1981 began sadly with the death in January of Princess Alice, the last surviving grand-daughter of Queen Victoria, at the age of 97. Her daughter had been bridesmaid to the Queen Mother who, with the Queen, now attended the Princess' funeral at Windsor (left). The following month brought the engagement of the Prince of Wales and the Queen Mother rejoiced with the rest of the nation at their wedding in July. Two other grandsons – Prince Edward (below) and Prince Andrew (bottom picture) – accompanied her on her travels that day. (Opposite page, below) entering St Paul's Cathedral with the Queen, Prince Philip and Prince Edward before the service. In November 1981, the Queen Mother inaugurated a new building at Lloyds of London (opposite page, top) by pulling a lever which started the first flow of cement.

things were at their most harrowing, the daily toll in life, limb, property and morale which the war exacted, continued their seemingly unending programme of hastily-arranged, ill-prepared but utterly spontaneous visits. When they were not surveying the ruins of Coventry, Hull, Portsmouth, Bath or Manchester they were inspecting the British war effort in every department, from ammunition factories to first aid posts and from defence command centres to local air raid shelters. Usually the King wore the uniform of one or other of the armed services, while the Queen dressed plainly, but impeccably, a combination which befitted the austerity-ridden circumstances as well as the morale-raising objectives of her missions. Nowhere were they any longer remotely unpopular: everywhere, vast crowds emerged from side streets and the wreckage of decent homes to reciprocate the royal gesture, and it was on occasions like those that the Queen initiated what we now take for granted as the walkabout. Harold Nicolson

spotted it during their visit to Sheffield in January 1941: "When the car stops, the Queen nips out into the snow and goes straight into the middle of the crowd and starts talking to them. For a moment or two they just gaze and gape in astonishment. But then they all start talking at once: 'Hi! Your Majesty! Look here! . . .'"

Winston Churchill was later to rhapsodise somewhat fulsomely over the effect the Queen had upon her husband's subjects on these sometimes depressing tours – "Many an aching heart found solace in her gracious smile" – but in the context of the heavy protocol which had for most of the century tended to distance the Crown from its people, the royal progresses offered a welcome glimmer of hope and even purpose during those painfully desperate early war years. Nor were they isolated examples of the Queen's concern for Britain's spiritual uplift. She made full and frequent use of the radio, using the precedents set by George V and particularly Edward VIII to drive home messages of encouragement to housewives,

those who played surrogate parents to evacuated children, nurses and medical volunteers. She stressed the importance of maintaining the family unit while home life was under pressure: "We must see to it," she told the women of Britain in 1940, "that our homes do not lose those very qualities which make them the background, as well as the joy of our lives." She also broadcast a message, in French, to the women of occupied France in 1940, and she did not forget the importance of American assistance, crucial even before the United States entered the war the following year. In a radio appeal to the women of America for continuing help in the hour of crisis, the Queen said, "To us in the time of tribulation you have surely shown the compassion which has for two thousand years been the mark of the good neighbour." Eleanor Roosevelt thought the speech "perfect in every way" and that it had done "a great amount of good." And it was the Queen who invited Mrs Roosevelt to Buckingham Palace in 1942 to stay before touring Britain to inspect women's war work and the activities of various American groups. Mrs Roosevelt accepted the invitation, saying, "It will be a pleasure to see you again," and when they met at Paddington Station the Queen assured her guests that "we welcome you with all our hearts." They got on well together, the Queen praising the spirit of the Londoner (echoing a previous remark: "They deserve a better world"), and consoling herself that the only apparent benefit of the East End bombing was that new houses would ultimately replace the old back-to-back slums. In that light one wonders what had passed between them when, after her second visit in 1945 to lunch with the Royal Family at Buckingham Palace, Mrs Roosevelt attributed to them the distant, unenthusiastic description of "nice people, but so far removed from life, it seems."

Mrs Roosevelt was not the only eminent foreign wartime visitor to Britain: several European heads of State had fled from the Germans in May and June 1940. The King's uncle, the ageing King Haakon VII of Norway

arrived with his son and heir, the present King Olav V, and took up residence at various country houses, including one of Sandringham's many outposts. Queen Wilhelmina of the Netherlands, a cousin of Queen Mary's sister-in-law Princess Alice of Athlone, came to lead a resistance government in exile shortly after her daughter, Princess Juliana, and her family stopped over on their way to Canada. They bought with them their ten-month-old daughter Princess Irene, for whom Queen Elizabeth stood as godmother when she was christened in the as yet unscathed chapel of Buckingham Palace shortly before their departure for North America in June 1940. The Grand Duchess Charlotte of

The Queen Mother's life is now a combination of old memories and new experiences. She remembered Flanagan and Allen, one of her favourite music hall duos, at a performance of Underneath the Arches *in London in March 1982 (below left), meeting Chesney Allen (left) only months before his death aged 88. (Opposite page, top and following page) with the Sultan of Oman the same month, during his State Visit to Britain. The Queen Mother's continuing rapport with the younger generation is illustrated by her welcome by Prince Andrew, a naval trainee at RAF Leeming at the time of her visit in 1980 (below), and in the christening day picture of her youngest great-grandchild, Prince William (opposite page, below).*

Luxemburg became another refugee in England and in 1941 King Peter of Yugoslavia and King George II of Greece joined her. Some of the visitors brought with them stories and rumours of Hitler's plans to capture the King and Queen but life went on as normally as the circumstances allowed at Buckingham Palace where a massive air raid shelter, generously proportioned, gas-proofed and made of solid concrete was installed. Diplomatic business went on there as before, as did the periodic Investitures, much increased in number owing to additional gallantry awards – in fact, almost 35,000 decorations were received at the Palace throughout the duration of the War. Meanwhile, in the Blue Drawing Room the Queen presided at twice-weekly sewing circles in which members of the Household and other Palace staff knitted and sewed clothes and comforts for servicemen as well as surgical dressings for the Red Cross. On a wider plane the King and Queen continued to attend State Openings of Parliament (though in cars rather than carriages), together with dedication and thanksgiving services at Westminster Abbey and St Paul's Cathedral, and the Queen was particularly keen to visit the lunchtime music concerts at the National Gallery, in spite of the risk of air raids at short notice.

Behind the scenes, however, the worst was being anticipated. Quite apart from the comparatively tame business of maintaining a Home Guard –

special visits from the cast of *ITMA* to which on one occasion the Queen invited 500 soldiers from a local barracks.

It was at Windsor that the Queen experienced one of mercifully few really horrific incidents. It had little directly to do with the War, then in its third year, except that the other party involved was a deserter from the Army. He had hidden behind a curtain in the Queen's bedroom in the Castle, and jumped out at her as she came into the room, seizing her ankles and preventing her from moving. With the same coolness that characterised her daughter's reaction in similar circumstances forty years later, she persuaded the intruder to talk quietly about what transpired to be crushing personal problems before taking the opportunity to summon help. The effort of overcoming her terror on that occasion was tested again the following year when the King made a journey by air – still adventurous in peace-time, perilous in war – to North Africa. The Queen knew he hated flying and fretted for his peace of mind as well as for his safety. On this particular trip the plans went awry as fog interrupted landing arrangements at Malta and Gibraltar and the King's plane was reported in the most unexpected places. The Queen confessed to Queen Mary afterwards that "I paced up and down my room, staring at the telephone and imagining every kind of horror." In spite of this she gamely encouraged the King to accompany the Operation Overlord Command to Northern France when invasion was first mooted in July 1943 – but his Private Secretary poured cold water on that idea in its infancy.

No doubt the Queen's sense of foreboding in relation to her husband's safety was occasioned, or at any rate, heightened by the tragedy the previous August, of the death of the King's brother, Prince George Duke of Kent. The King and Queen were dining with the Duke and Duchess of Gloucester at Balmoral when the King was called away to receive the news that the Duke of Kent had been instantaneously killed when his RAF plane, flying from Invergordon

there was a special unit at Buckingham Palace itself – and discovering how to work stirrup pumps and perfecting gas-mask drill, the Queen learned to shoot to kill with the most up-to-date revolvers and rifles. That achievement gave her great pleasure and she told Harold Nicolson, "I shall not go down like the others" with such conviction that he wrote afterwards "We *shall* win: I know that."

The War was even less disruptive at Windsor, the King and Queen's week-end haven and their night-time headquarters when the Blitz-damaged Buckingham Palace was being repaired. Here, the two princesses continued with their lessons under the general supervision of the septuagenarian Clara Cooper-Knight who, scrupulous as ever, insisted that they should be properly dressed even before they went into their air-raid shelter! Royal Lodge's pink walls were now covered with camouflage paint, but it was here that the famous Windsor Castle entertainments – conceived through the fun-loving inspiration of the Queen herself – took shape in the form of Christmas pantomimes in which the princesses took part, and

to Iceland, crashed into a mountain-side in North-East Scotland – ironically for the Queen, on the Caithness estate of her close kinsman the Duke of Portland. As stunned as any member of the Royal Family was, she returned immediately to London with the King and it is said that she actually physically had to restrain the woefully distraught widow, Princess Marina, from throwing herself into the royal vault when the Duke's coffin was lowered into it at the end of the committal service at St George's Chapel Windsor. While it would have been almost improper for her to have voiced any complaint, the Queen must have mused bitterly on the personal anguish left by the senseless atrocities and quirkish misfortunes of war, for her brother-in-law's death was not her only casualty. Her nephew John Bowes-Lyon, the heir to the Strathmore and Kinghorne title, was killed in North Africa, another nephew, John Elphinstone came home wounded and a third nephew, later the fifth Earl of Granville, was twice wounded in battle. The family toll was nowhere

near as severe as in the previous conflict but it was enough to eliminate any trace of banality from her annual post-War visits to the Field of Remembrance and her attendances at the Festivals of Remembrance each November, and to invest them with meaning and not a little poignancy.

It was an agonisingly long haul from the turn of the tide in 1943 to the achievement of full European peace – and victory – in May 1945, but when it happened the "brief moment of rejoicing" was overwhelming. The Royal Family appeared on the Palace balcony whose tasselled drapes concealed the evidence of the bomb damage, against a backdrop of shattered and blacked-out casements. Prime Minister Churchill, who joined them there, was speechless with emotion at the honour of it. The King looked solemn as if inwardly grateful and relieved by the deliverance which had once seemed impossible. The Queen looked triumphant, her two daughters suddenly immensely grown-up. In the plethora of parades and processions that followed, there was none of that resentment which had soured at least one royal visit to the East End in 1940. Just as in 1941 the Queen had, according to President Roosevelt's Personal Assistant,

"It is very simple, this lying-in-state of a dead King . . ." So said Richard Dimbleby, the BBC's radio commentator in an articulate and moving description of the four-day vigil (left) at Westminster Hall, which culminated in King George VI's funeral at Windsor on 15th February, 1952. Officers of the Household Brigades and the Royal Bodyguard of Yeomen guarded the King's flag-draped coffin which bore the emblems of State and towered high above wreaths from his grieving widow and family. An even more poignant simplicity characterised the earlier, more domestic honour, when (above left) members of the King's estate staff stood at the four corners of the Royal coffin at St Mary Magdalene church within the confines of the Sandringham Estate where the King had died. The simple white wreath was from the new Queen and Princess Margaret; that on the coffin from the bereaved Queen Consort

"found it extremely difficult to find words to express her feelings towards the people of Britain – she thought their actions magnificent and that victory in the long run was sure," so now a celebrating Irishwoman in London's Commercial Road reciprocated with a blunter but equally articulate tribute: "I always was partial to royalty – and still am!"

The British Royal House, like most of the constitutional monarchies of Europe with the exception of Belgium, came through the War and its whirlwind aftermath dominated by the Soviet push from the East, not only unscathed but strengthened. It must have been with utter dismay that the King and Queen saw their distant relatives and fellow monarchs liquidated or bundled out of their eastern European lands as

Roumania, Bulgaria and Yugoslavia fell to Communist republicanism just as in 1918 Austria, Prussia and Russia had collapsed under the weight of humiliating defeats at the hands of their adversaries. In Greece the monarchy, which had never in the previous quarter century been sufficiently stable to increase its chances of survival, swayed this way and that at the mercy of politicians of the left and right, and the Italians wasted little time ridding themselves of King Victor Emmanuel III and his son of short reign, Umberto II.

But as the remaining western European monarchs returned from exile to their homelands, the British Royal Family were able to command the spontaneous affection and loyalty of the surging masses who surrounded Buckingham Palace, for having been with

them throughout the worst bombing and the privations of this most cataclysmic of wars. The Queen even received a poem from a lady in Chicago, praising her for "wearing your gayest gown, your bravest smile . . . when London Bridge was burning down," and Eleanor Roosevelt, ever the most dispassionate of commentators, averred that "in all my contacts with them I have gained the

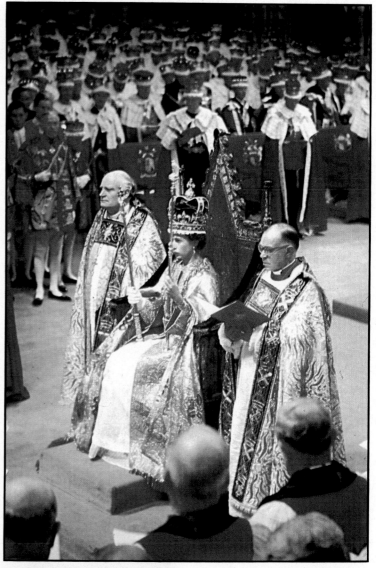

greatest respect for the King and Queen. Both of them are doing an extraordinarily outstanding job for the people. You admire their character and devotion to duty." Little wonder therefore, that the King and Queen found themselves the objects of such great tribute on the many occasions when the victory was celebrated. In nine of the most challenging years, particularly for sovereigns of such little previous first-hand experience, they had triumphed – and all by their own efforts.

It was all the more unfair, therefore, that when the opportunity came, as it now did, for consolidation and the luxury of looking back with some satisfaction on what had gone before, the King and Queen – particularly the Queen on whom the burden eventually fell – should have had such a hard time of it. The horror of war

The Coronation of the new Queen in Westminster Abbey on 2nd June 1953 was a family occasion in many respects. Members of her own family came to do homage to her, others watched from a gallery behind the plate-laden altar. A wider family was represented by the attendance of delegates from many constituents of a dying Empire and a growing Commonwealth. The armills, or bracelets, seen (left) among the Coronation regalia, were a gift from this family of nations. For the Queen Mother it was an occasion of memories; her attendance, following the precedent set by Queen Mary in 1937, was also a declaration of confidence in the new Queen who, from the first, showed herself to be very much her father's daughter. For a short while, the four-year-old Prince Charles was allowed into the Abbey to watch the proceedings, keeping his doting grandmother busy with questions.

The Queen Mother remained tactfully unobtrusive during the intense activity of her daughter's early years as Queen. There were visits abroad – Bermuda in 1953 (far right), Denmark in 1957 (below and opposite page, centre left), Holland in 1958 (right) – engagements at home: (bottom right) in May 1961; (centre) in November 1962; (opposite page, bottom left) leaving the National Gallery in 1962 and (centre) leaving St Paul's in 1961 with Prince Philip after the service of the Order of St Michael and St George.

Princess Margaret seemed a busy woman too, especially after her marriage in 1960 – (left) with her husband at St Paul's Cathedral in May 1961. (Above right) Princess Margaret as Chancellor of Keele University in July 1962; (opposite page, centre) at a wedding at Westminster Abbey in 1962; (far right) in July 1961. The Queen Mother joined the Snowdons and

Prince Andrew (opposite page, top left) en route for the Trooping in June 1965. By this time, the Queen Mother's senior grandson was within months of his 18th birthday, and the following year he began his three-year course of study at Trinity College Cambridge (opposite page, top right) where the public spotlight began to turn inexorably on him.

gave way to an uneasy peace, and one which at home brought the long trial of austerity as the new Labour Government wrestled to reconcile their sincerely-held Socialist principles with the need to put the economy back on its feet. This was not helped by the appalling winter of 1946/47 when shortages of food and fuel were aggravated by months of freezing weather and almost insurmountable transport difficulties. The embarrassment thus felt by the King and Queen, for whom a visit to South Africa had been planned many months beforehand, was acute as they

realised the irony of their being in warm, sunny climes while their fellow countrymen were suffering perpetual and worsening assaults on their welfare. The King referred to his dilemma several times in his speeches during that tour, and the Queen confirmed his unease: "it is doubly hard for Bertie, who feels he should be at home," she wrote to Queen Mary. "We think of home all the time."

The visit, bursting with sunshine, celebration and song, was famous for the fact that Princess Elizabeth and Princess Margaret – then twenty and sixteen respectively – joined their parents for the first time on a major official tour. It is now particularly remembered for the elder daughter's dedication of her "whole life, whether it be long or short" to the service of the peoples of the Commonwealth and Empire, on her twenty-first birthday that April. Already it seemed that the King and Queen, conscious of their own sad lack of preparation for the Throne, were schooling their daughter for the time – though little did they suspect its proximity – when she would take over the reins of

Some private moments with the Queen Mother's family. (Centre) her grandchildren with their parents at Clarence House, Summer 1951. (Bottom centre) Prince Charles takes his sister out in 1954. (Left) watching Prince Philip at polo, Windsor 1956. (Below) the family at Windsor Castle, 1957. (Bottom left) the Queen and Princess Anne, Windsor 1959. (Centre left) the Queen with Prince Edward, leaving King's Cross Station for Balmoral, August 1964, and again (bottom right) with Prince Andrew two years later.

constitutional power.
Yet there was another, more subtle reason for the Princess' inclusion on the tour. She had already developed an affection for a young naval lieutenant, Prince Philip of Greece who, like her, was a great-great-grandchild of Queen Victoria and thus her third cousin. It is still a matter of some conjecture as to when this mutual

attachment was first conceived. Although the couple met during a visit which the King and Queen made to Dartmouth in 1939, it seems clear, especially for the thirteen-year-old Princess, no ulterior motive existed, except possibly in the mind of Lord Louis Mountbatten, Prince Philip's uncle, who had for many years been rumoured to have pressed the claims of members of his family for the hand of successive heirs to the Throne. The Duke of Edinburgh has pooh-poohed the notion that there was some long term plan to match him with the heiress presumptive, and in particular has dismissed

Chips Channon's well-aimed guess as early as 1942 that "he is to be our future Prince Consort, and that is why he is in our Navy." It was however more than evident to an eagle-eyed Press that the look which Prince Philip gave Princess Elizabeth while taking her fur jacket from her as she entered Westminster Abbey for the wedding of Mountbatten's daughter Patricia in 1946 proclaimed something deeper than his natural flair for impeccable, gentlemanly behaviour.

It was a good guess, and indeed it seems from later correspondence between the King and his daughter that she

(Top) Prince Charles' long held affection for the Mountbattens has early origins: they took him to Gibraltar to welcome the Queen and Prince Philip back from their Commonwealth Tour in 1954. (Right and centre left) two of the more informal family photographs taken in the grounds of Balmoral to mark the Queen and Prince Philip's Silver Wedding in 1972. In the mid-'sixties and 1970s the Queen Mother acquired the nickname "Queen Gran," and from the pictures (above and centre right) both taken in 1970, it is not difficult to see why.

The Queen Mother has seen both daughters and two grandchildren married, though Princess Margaret, engaged in February 1960 (top right and opposite page) divorced Lord Snowdon in 1978. Princess Elizabeth's wedding in November 1947 (opposite page) to Lieutenant Philip Mountbatten brightened a dull post-war Britain, while the engagements of Princess Anne to Lieutenant Mark Phillips in May 1973, (bottom centre) and of Prince Charles to Lady Diana Spencer in February 1981 (right and below) prompted widespread popularity. (Bottom, left and right) Princess Elizabeth and her husband in Malta in 1949.

had wanted a fairly early engagement. But arrangements for the South African tour were too well advanced to allow for Princess Elizabeth's withdrawal, as she would no doubt have preferred, and it appears that the Queen was instrumental in persuading her to give her feelings time to settle. Shortly after her wedding in November 1947, the Princess wrote to her mother that she fully appreciated the wisdom of waiting before becoming

engaged, and another example of the Queen's tactful and wise influence as a concerned mother came to a successful conclusion. This first post-war royal wedding, though restricted by

Of the thirteen foreign tours Princess Margaret undertook in the 1950s, five involved British Commonwealth countries such as Kenya, Zanzibar (above and right) in 1956, and Canada (far right) in 1958. In 1960, the Queen received President de Gaulle on a State Visit to England – the first by a French president since the War. (Top centre) the Queen arriving at Covent Garden for a gala performance in the President's honour.

The Queen Mother pursued her own programme of journeys abroad with visits to Rhodesia in 1953, 1957 and 1960, Canada in 1954 and 1958, Australasia in 1958 and East Africa in 1959. In addition she visited France and Italy.

the observance of austerity measures which even for the Royal Family were still in force, provided a rare moment of colour in a grey world. Out came the gleaming royal carriages, and the bride who, we are told, had to save up her ration coupons for months in advance to obtain enough material for her wedding dress, contrasted sweetly – ensconced in its soft white – with the blaze of scarlet and black from the uniforms of the troops lining the streets of London. For the first time since the beginning of hostilities the soldiers were out of khaki, and the capital saw ceremonial in full colour as it had not done for almost a decade.

For all that, these November

festivities were a mere foretaste of another celebration soon to come. On 26th April 1948, the King and Queen reached their Silver Wedding anniversary, and on a bright and sunny spring Monday they rode in carriage procession to St Paul's Cathedral for a thanksgiving service. It was not just the sky that was blue: as if in tribute to the Queen's favourite colour, Princess Elizabeth wore a china blue dress with a blue fox cape, and Princess Margaret – now a rising eighteen-year-old – was dressed in a deep blue outfit. The Queen matched her daughters with a silver-blue full length gown with a sweeping train – a model of the New Look era which better times were ushering into the fashion world. On her dress appeared the Order of the Garter and two family orders, and a large, fluffy boa was slung warmly round her neck. With her now famed, matronly smile and gracious wave, she sat beside the King, who had chosen naval uniform for the day, as through the deafening cheers of the heavily-lined streets and to the distant thunder of gun salutes and bray of trumpet fanfares they reached St Paul's where a capacity congregation took part in the service.

Back at Buckingham Palace, 150 guests were entertained to a three-course luncheon, and a large cake bearing the coats of arms of the King and Queen was cut. That evening they toured the East End, encountering street after street blocked by cheering crowds who swarmed round the royal car, even throwing flowers through the window onto the Queen's lap. The 21-mile drive was such a success that they were half an hour late returning to the Palace, arriving only just in time to give a pre-arranged broadcast to the nation. The King, quietly grateful for the day's show of intense popular loyalty,

1961 saw the birth of the Queen Mother's fourth grandchild – the first son of Princess Margaret. David, Viscount Linley, seen (top and above left) with his parents and grandmother as Princess Margaret left Clarence House a month later, was born there on 3rd November. His sister Sarah (above, on her christening day) was born in 1964, one of the four royal babies born that year, of whom James Ogilvy, son of Princess Alexandra (top left) was the first – born on Leap Year's Day. The Gloucesters produced their first two children in the 1970s: (left) with their second child Davina at her christening in 1978.

struggled to express his appreciation: it was as if he now knew how almost bewildered his father had been at the acclaim his people gave him at the Silver Jubilee. The Queen joined in the broadcast, emphasising her concern for those still facing the privations of post-war life: "My heart goes out to all who are living in uncongenial surroundings and who are longing for the time when they will have a home of their own. The world today is longing to find the secret of community, and all married lives are in a sense communities in miniature."

Certain it was that she had found

The Queen Mother clearly enjoying the large family gathering after the christening of Peter Phillips, Princess Anne's first child, at Buckingham Palace in December 1977 (top and above left). Prince William of Wales, born on 21st June 1982, emerged from hospital in Paddington on the 22nd, when the Queen Mother first saw him. A popular recent addition to the Royal Family has been Princess Michael of Kent, whose son Frederick was christened at St. James's Palace in July 1979 (top left).

The Queen (below left) attending a banquet during her State Visit to France in April 1957; (bottom picture) leaving the Saudi-Arabian Embassy in London after a banquet in 1967; (right) on a State Visit to Yugoslavia in 1972; (bottom centre) hosting Commonwealth Prime Ministers at Buckingham Palace in 1977. The Queen is seen (below right) at the film première of Waterloo in October 1970, and visited the Tutankhamun exhibition in London in 1972 (bottom right).

On the page opposite, the Queen attends Claridge's as the guest of the Grand Duke of Luxemburg (bottom left) in June 1972, and is joined by other members of her family during the King of Denmark's visit in 1967 (bottom right) and the Queen of the Netherlands' State Visit in 1974 (top): the Queen Mother is seen with Prince Bernhardt (centre left). Two film premières for Princess Margaret: in October 1977 (centre right) and in March 1981 (centre).

the community spirit in the Londoners that day. "We were dumbfounded by our reception," she said. "It spurs us on to further efforts." Often the fêting of the monarch, as Churchill once wryly observed, provides a means of expressing general popular contentment, and even the Royal Family's latest recruit, the Duke of Edinburgh, admitted after a visit with Princess Elizabeth to France, that only part of the acclaim may have been directed at them personally. But there could be no doubt that, with little enough to cheer about, the British people were truly expressing through their celebration of the Silver Wedding their affection

hardening of the arteries set in. The danger of gangrene presented itself and at one time it was feared that the King might have to have a leg amputated. The development could not have come at a more trying time – Princess Elizabeth was then in the advanced stages of her first pregnancy – but the Queen was resigned to bearing much of the burden of worry herself. She gave instructions that her daughter was not to be informed of the full extent of her father's condition, and during the increasing pressure of duties that her deputising for the King entailed, she radiated that outward, pleasurable calm which the experience of previous years

for their modest, dutiful King and the wife who, with what one of the King's equerries called her "steely will" had made everything possible for him during the previous twenty-five years.

As it happened, the Silver Wedding marked the end of an all too brief period of unallayed happiness, for the next four years were beset by the anxieties and upsets caused by a repetitive and steady deterioration in the King's health. By the end of 1948 he was out of action with severe circulatory trouble and

had taught her to maintain, no matter how hostile the circumstances. It was particularly distressing to be deprived of Princess Elizabeth's company the following year, when she went to join her husband in Malta where he was serving with the Royal Navy. The King responded well to treatment and, in the cautious optimism of the New Year, undertook a few engagements. By March, however, the blood-flow to his legs was found to be still obstructed, and further treatment – a lumbar sympathectomy – proved necessary and for the time being successful. He began to resume a gentle programme of duties, but already he was beginning to

Whether at the ballet, the theatre, the opera or the cinema, the Queen Mother, like her two daughters, revels with the best of them in the sparkle of a glittering evening occasion.

look painfully thin, a prematurely ageing man with wispy, greying hair – a shadow, it seems with hindsight, of worse things to come. Even so, he was able to enjoy life and at a cocktail party of the Duke of

Kent's Buckinghamshire home in June 1950, he was said to be looking "much younger than the Duke of Windsor," while the Queen, stoically accepting what was and what had to be, continued to withstand the trials of those waning years. She "looked sublime," according to Chips Channon in 1951. "I really marvelled at her self-

while his parents were absent from home on successive official duties abroad, the Queen continued to act in public as if untroubled by any doubt about the King's health. Even on that January day in 1952, when they both walked onto the tarmac at London Airport to see Princess Elizabeth and her husband off on a Commonwealth tour which

the King was too ill to make himself, the Queen kept up that cheerful, almost chatty spirit which had characterised her public appearances in all the harrowing preceding months. But she knew, and the pitifully preoccupied look on the King's face made it clear that he knew too, that this would be his last sight of his daughter. It was a

cold and windy day, and the King, gaunt, staring, swamped in a heavy great-coat yet bare-headed, strained for a last lingering look of the departing Argonaut aircraft. Then he made his leaden-hearted way back to Buckingham Palace, and thence eventually to Sandringham. It was there that he spent 5th February shooting hares at

possession."

As we now know, she was to need all the self-possession she could muster that year. In May, soon after the King had in the presence of the entire Royal Family opened the Festival of Britain, he fell ill with influenza, and an inspection of the left lung, which had been severely affected by catarrhal inflammation, exposed a malignant growth. In an operating theatre specially set up at Buckingham Palace, he underwent a delicate operation to remove his lung by resection, and throughout that agonising treatment and the week of anxiety that followed, the Queen hardly left his side.

Gradually, the King regained his strength, but by then the Queen knew that cancer had taken its hold and would in a matter of months claim her husband's life. Sharing that information with her daughters but, naturally, keeping it from the three-year-old Prince Charles, who was a frequent and welcome young guest at Buckingham Palace

Flitcham, on the Sandringham Estate, while the Queen and Princess Margaret motored across Norfolk for a cruise on the Broads and a visit to the painter Edward Seago, joining the King back at the Big House that evening. And it was there too that in the small hours of the following day he died, discovered at daybreak by his valet who had brought his early morning tea.

To the Queen, whose long expectation of the inevitable could not soften the crush of grief when the blow fell, his death marked not only the loss of a husband but also of a position and a way of life. The relentless and unquestioning machinery of dynastic succession which had already operated at the unwatched hour of the King's demise, took its automatic course and Princess Elizabeth was, in her absence, proclaimed Queen, succeeding her mother as first lady in the land. We are not told whether, on her arrival back at Buckingham Palace the following day, the new Queen was curtsied to by her mother, as Queen Mary did at Marlborough House that afternoon – "her old granny and subject must be the first to do her homage," – but the point does not need forcing. From then on Queen Elizabeth, adopting the title of Queen Mother as Queen Alexandra had done in 1910, took second place. Nevertheless, the obsequies kept her, perhaps unwillingly, in the forefront of public attention – "that most valiant woman," as Churchill described her, widowed at the unfairly early age of 51, draped in black for the succession of ceremonial which accompanied the transportation of her husband's remains from Sandringham to London and then, after a four-day Lying-in-State at Westminster Hall, to Windsor Castle for the committal. The Queen Mother followed the coffin all the way, and at its resting places a simple white wreath was placed upon it bearing the equally simple, personal message, "Darling Bertie, from his always loving Elizabeth," proclaiming in one of those rare examples of the exposition of private royal thoughts to public view, the undying affection which had

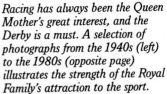

Racing has always been the Queen Mother's great interest, and the Derby is a must. A selection of photographs from the 1940s (left) to the 1980s (opposite page) illustrates the strength of the Royal Family's attraction to the sport.

made their joint lives full of meaning and purpose. The public too responded with shows of respect for the late King and demonstrations of sympathy for his widow. "Your concern for me has upheld me in my sorrow," she gratefully declared, "and how proud you have made me by your wonderful tributes to my dear husband."

The suddenness of the event, dramatised by those final, appalling photographs and newsreel films of the dying monarch, has invested the death of King George VI with a significance more macabre and consequences more deplorable than even his widow would, at the safe distance which time now offers, consider justified today. And however unfair it seemed that he should now be dead she did not, as some of her predecessors had, allow the proprieties of mourning to consume her natural instinct for life as it must best be lived. But she knew when to take a back seat, and was probably more than willing to do so as the new Queen assumed her father's mantle of sovereignty. The Queen Mother's first preoccupation was that of moving house – a complicated business which Queen Alexandra, jealously attached to Buckingham Palace, made much of when her turn came to leave after King Edward VII's death, and which even Queen Mary was in no great hurry to proceed with in 1936. In events, the Queen Mother's removal took some fifteen months to complete, involving as it did a

was built by John Nash for King William IV when he was Duke of Clarence, in 1825, almost forty years after he had first occupied a house on the same site. Queen Victoria's mother had lived there for twenty years, and it eventually became the home – though not much lived in – of Arthur, Duke of Connaught until his death, as Queen Victoria's last surviving son, in 1942. After serving as a Red Cross headquarters for five years, it was taken over in 1949 and much modernised, as White Lodge had been in its day, by Princess Elizabeth and the Duke of Edinburgh, whose second child Princess Anne was born there in August 1950. The Queen Mother has succeeded, as no other royal

convenient exchange of residences with her elder daughter, who for the previous three years had lived at Clarence House.

Clarence House and Queen Elizabeth the Queen Mother have become almost synonymous in the last thirty years, just as Marlborough House had been with Queen Mary. It is in fact part of St James's Palace, which it effectively adjoins, and has been described – in a rather vain attempt to make it sound remotely comparable to anything in the more common run of houses – as two back-to-back houses joined into one. It

The Duke of Windsor's death in May 1972 brought his widow to England. Previously, only an attendance at a family ceremony in Queen Mary's memory in 1967 (top) provided some evidence of a thaw in the uneasy relationship.

For the Queen Mother, 1972 brought unhappiness, with the deaths of King Frederick of Denmark, of Alexander Ramsay (husband of the former Princess Patricia of Connaught) and of Prince William of Gloucester, killed in an air race that August. This talented, open-minded Prince (top pictures, as a teenager with his family at Barnwell) would otherwise have succeeded as Duke of Gloucester. His father (centre pictures, with Princess Alice) outlived him, and was given a military funeral at Windsor in June 1974 (bottom).

occupant this century, in making it the perfect permanent London home. Although it houses administrative offices, and despite the noble display of royal insignia outside – even the lamp-posts are surmounted by miniature crowns – its cream-painted exterior and heavy, highly-polished mahogany doors enclose a spacious, restful house which in design, furnishing and ornamentation is *very* Queen Mother. A plethora of silver

trophies chart her satisfyingly successful thirty-five-year old career as a race-horse owner; glass-fronted cabinets house her collection of Red Anchor period Chelsea china, accumulated over many years; her weakness for Regency wine coasters is revealed, and the huge mirrors and chandeliers, the heavy velvet drapes and valances at the windows add luxurious style to this otherwise homely building. Her private sitting-room sports a marble mantlepiece built, before the house itself, in the mid-18th century, but the Queen Mother's taste for the more modern expressions of art are epitomised by the wide variety of pictures she has collected: Sickert, the English impressionist, she is very fond of; L.S. Lowry she discovered before most other people did; Edward Seago is well patronised by the Royal Family, and all have a place here. Alongside are such occasional paintings as a portrait of King George VI investing Princess Elizabeth with the Order of the Garter, and an uncompleted

portrait of the Queen Mother herself by Augustus John: he started it during the War, but never finished it, and when he died the directors of a company who took over his premises found the portrait and presented it to her. "It has cheered me up no end," she said after she received it.

In the meantime, the Queen Mother had busied herself with acquiring another home, and something different from anything she had lived in before. It says a great deal for her vigour and search for new life amid the desolation of widowhood that she was in the mood to spot a good prospect when it presented itself, and it was during a short holiday at the

Caithness home of her friends Commander and Lady Doris Vyner, not long after the King's death, that she heard about the proposed demolition of Barrogill Castle, built four hundred years previously by the Earl of Caithness. Spontaneously she deplored its threatened passing, and decided to acquire it as much as an act of historical and architectural preservation (the Castle has a barrel-vaulted ceiling) as for herself. A long period of restoration followed: the interiors were renovated and filled with furniture which she personally collected almost

The Badminton Horse Trials have a magnetic attraction for the Queen Mother, who attends every April, usually with a large representation from her family. These pictures, taken in 1972, 1973 and 1977 show her with her two daughters and all six grandchildren, except for Princess Anne, a regular competitor when not prevented by the demands of motherhood.

piece by piece, the facilities were modernised, and the gardens gradually persuaded into shape with the front lawn sporting two trees which King Edward VII and Queen Alexandra, then Prince and Princess of Wales, had planted in the 1870's.

The Queen Mother restored not only the building but also its original name, the Castle of Mey. And despite – perhaps because of – its isolated position on the coldest of north-east coasts, it has become her place of pilgrimage since she first moved in at the end of October 1955. Once upon a time she used to spend two or three short holidays a year there, but now restricts herself to a single visit, usually in the company of half a dozen friends, during the few weeks of the summer when everything is at its best. The woods to the front of the Castle are in full leaf, bounded by the Thurso river where she once fished for salmon; the coastal views of the Pentland Firth to the rear are clear, with distant vistas of the Orkneys on the finest days; and the weather allows her to take a breezy consitutional over the cliffs or on the beaches, where she might collect shells for the cosy rooms of the house itself. Within the four high brick walls shelters the archetypal cottage garden – a large-scale affair stretching over two acres – where everything from soft fruits to herbs, and begonias to clematis, are reared and nursed into maturity ready for her annual visit. The garden

is now open briefly to the public who can see for themselves the profusion of snapdragon and sweet pea, gooseberry and geranium, apple and artichoke – a rich pattern of colour and ripeness amid the bleak, peaty landscape.

The year 1953 opened hardly more promisingly than 1952, with disastrous floods along the east coast of England and the last illness and death of 84-year-old Queen Mary in March. She died within ten weeks of that momentous occasion for which she would have wished to be spared but which, anticipating her own passing, she instructed should not be cancelled as the result of any mourning on her

account. The Coronation of Queen Elizabeth II outshone almost every previous royal event in terms of panache, colour and, thanks to the advent of popular television, significance. The gradual trend over the years in favour of greater media participation in major royal events made it almost certain that the Coronation would be televised, and when the Coronation Committee, chaired by the Duke of Edinburgh, announced that it would, there was an immediate rush to buy or hire sets especially for the occasion. It was good to feel that anyone, anywhere, whether they were sitting in public houses with their hats on or not, could be within effective reach of the grand ceremonial which would confirm the Queen Mother's 27-year-old daughter as Queen of Great Britain.

The Queen Mother was able to

see at first hand, during her many drives through London in the months before the Coronation, the progress of the preparations for this great event. Like Queen Mary before her, she decided that she too would attend the ceremony to watch her daughter crowned, and she arrived at Westminster Abbey on the morning of 2nd June 1953, dignified and regal in her own procession. Her entry was, invidiously but inevitably, compared with that in 1937 of Queen Mary, and was generally thought to be less imposing – but as events later proved the difference was not a question of

presence but of style. The following years would show that the warmer, more spontaneous and kindly public attitude of the Queen Mother would be much more appropriate and appreciated in the new age than Queen Mary's thoroughly regal, almost imperious formality. At least some continuity characterised the Queen Mother's appearance – she wore a magnificent train which had in fact been used by Queen Mary at the 1937 Coronation; it was trimmed with ermine and carried by four young pages. As on her Silver Wedding day, she wore the Order of the Garter which her husband had given to her on his forty-first birthday, only three days after his

One of 1972's more joyous occasions was the Silver Wedding of the Queen and Prince Philip in November. Almost fifty years after her own wedding, the Queen Mother attended the Thanksgiving Service in Westminster Abbey with Princess Margaret, Lord Snowdon and their children (below), and the Queen's own family (right and below right). She joined them for the mayoral luncheon at the Guildhall afterwards (bottom pictures). An occasion of State which nevertheless carried all the familiar signs of a happy family celebration was the Silver Jubilee in 1977 (opposite page) which the Queen Mother attended, wearing a bright yellow outfit. In deference to her own personal memories, the official celebrations took place not on 6th February – the anniversary of King George VI's death – but early the following June.

House to resume her every-day life. She was not without company, for in addition to the many friends who became part of her paid and unpaid staff, Princess Margaret, then in her 23rd year and unmarried, lived in. But even at the time of the Coronation there were difficulties for the Queen Mother from this quarter, and she found that all her reserves of discretion, understanding, patience and inner convictions were required all over again for what became universally known as the Townsend Affair.

Group Captain Peter Townsend had, since just after the War, been an equerry to the King and a trusted member of the Royal Household with whom he travelled, by and large, wherever the King and Queen travelled. When the King died, his widow

Accession, as well as the personal orders bearing miniature portraits of King George V, King George VI and the new Queen. On her head she wore the circlet which had formed the base of the crown she had worn in 1937.

Much as the Queen Mother was prepared to remain quietly in the background, there was a brief period during the Abbey ceremony when she almost upstaged her daughter. It had been decided that the young Prince Charles, the four-and-a-half-year-old Duke of Cornwall, should visit the Abbey to watch part of the ceremony, and his grandmother – "a figure of love and affection for young and old alike," as he has since described

her – agreed that he could sit with her at the centre of the front row of the Royal Gallery. His arrival – a dapper young man in white silks and slicked-down hair – was furtive enough, but when he began pointing and plaguing his grandmother with questions, her patient attempts to answer them as inconspicuously as possible sent the television and film cameras all pointing her way. And when he disappeared from view, the photographers joined in recording the fun as the Queen Mother and Princess Margaret searched for him in the dark recesses of the gallery.

When the long Coronation festivities were over, the Queen Mother settled into Clarence

requested him to become Comptroller of her Household, based at Clarence House, supervising the internal organisation of the Queen Mother's new home and offices. His admiration and affection for her was "like everybody's, boundless," particularly for "her graciousness, her gaiety and her unfailing thoughtfulness for others." He has since been particularly complimentary about her reaction to the news, broken to her by Princess Margaret in February 1953, that he and the Princess were in love.

The complication was that Townsend had just been through a divorce from his first wife Rosemary who, that month, married Philip de Lazslo, the · son of one of the Queen Mother's favourite portrait painters during her years as Duchess of York. For the Queen Mother especially, it was an ironic blow, considering the events of seventeen years before, but one that even in the slightly more liberated atmosphere of

the new Elizabethan age had to be coped with in the most delicate manner. Townsend, who of course knew the Queen Mother well, did not seem at all surprised by her charitable reaction and, bearing in mind the tenor of her upbringing and her natural consideration for others – "I have never heard an ugly word pass that child's lips," Lady Strathmore had once told Princess Marie-Louise of

Like many of her previous birthdays, the Queen Mother's 75th and 80th birthdays were marked by the issue of official photographs. Norman Parkinson, one of her favourite photographers, took all four pictures on these pages. The formal ones show Her Majesty wearing the same pearl and diamond necklace and honeycomb tiara, while the less formal emphasise the homely surroundings and (right) continuing close family ties. The two pictures below commemorate the 75th birthday; the others were taken for her 80th.

Schleswig-Holstein – nor should we. According to Townsend the Queen Mother "listened with characteristic understanding. I imagine that her immediate, and natural reaction was 'this simply cannot be'. But thoughtful as ever for the feelings of others, she did not hurt us by saying so. Without a sign that she felt angered or outraged – or on the other hand that she acquiesced – the Queen Mother was never anything but considerate in her attitude toward me. Indeed, she never hurt either of us throughout the whole difficult affair, behaving always with regard for us both, for which I felt all the more grateful because of my own responsibility."

She even agreed that there was no need for Townsend to leave Clarence House, and she invited him to stay on in his current position. But it appears (though the full story of machination behind Palace walls has not been satisfactorily exposed) that

Princess Margaret's departure for a tour of Rhodesia, and a final (for the time being) meeting took place, emotionally, at Clarence House. During it, the Queen Mother exhibited once again her sympathy and understanding (and Townsend "blessed her for her exquisite tact") by leaving the room early and allowing the young people alone together for a few precious minutes.

The story did not end there for when, after two years, he came back to Britain, he and the Princess found their love as strong as ever. By that time,

The Queen wears distinctive Canadian insignia in place of the usual family orders on these two occasions (top) during her 1977 visit to Canada. (Centre) the Queen Mother and some of her immediate family with the King of Sweden during his State Visit in 1975. With them at Holyroodhouse are the Duke and Duchess of Gloucester, Earl Mountbatten and Sweden's Princess Margrethe with her husband. (Far left) the Queen and Prince Philip with President and Madame Giscard d'Estaing of France at Buckingham Palace in 1977. (Left) the Queen entertained the Amir of Bahrain to a banquet on board Britannia *during her Gulf Tour, February 1979.*

her response did not accord with decisions being taken by or on behalf with the Queen's Private Secretary. With the American newspapers running continual stories about Princess Margaret's liaison and concocting the usual wave of preposterous sensations on the subject, preparations to sweep the dirt under the carpet were already under way, and by the end of June 1953 Townsend had been sent to Brussels to continue his RAF advisory career with the British Embassy there. His transfer coincided with the Queen Mother's and

(Below) the Queen attending a reception during her State Visit to Yugoslavia in October 1972. (Bottom) the Queen Mother chatting to Princess Anne before a State banquet at Windsor. (Right) the Queen Mother and (far right) the Queen arriving for the State banquet given by King Khalid of Saudi Arabia in June 1981.

however, the full weight of the Establishment was marshalled against what by then had become a prospective marriage, and after several meetings with the Prime Minister, the Archbishop of Canterbury and other advisors, Princess Margaret reluctantly but resignedly issued a public statement announcing that "mindful of the Church's teaching that marriage is indissoluble" she would not after all marry her suitor of almost three years.

That was in October 1955, and throughout the entire period of the turmoil in which her younger daughter found herself, the Queen Mother's support and advice was by all accounts constant, wise and, in the context of the unfavourable circumstances of the day, probably correct. In events, her comforting presence seemed to be a soothing influence on the Princess, whose official duties continued with remarkable

aplomb and even verve, despite the persistent attempt by the Press of Britain, Europe and the United States to link her name permanently with any one of the dozens of male members of the "Margaret Set." Eventually she found her long-sought happiness with Antony Armstrong-Jones, one of the Court photographers since 1956, whose portraits of the Queen, Prince Charles, Princess Anne and Princess Margaret herself had become much admired for their pin-sharp clarity and imaginative style.

The romance between them was almost as controversial as the Townsend affair, with hot gossip on the Bohemian life-style of the artistic types with whom Armstrong-Jones was thought to be associated, raised eye-brows at the fact that he had two step-mothers in addition to his own,

The Queen Mother wearing bright blue at a flower show in 1976 (below and below left). She wore a light blue and white outfit for a service in St Paul's in 1977 (below right) and a similar flower-patterned dress, coat and hat for her 78th birthday a year later. Almost exactly a year after that she was installed as Lord Warden of the Cinque Ports at Dover and in spite of bleak August weather, she was in high spirits as (opposite page, top right) she shook hands with a long line of local dignitaries. A persistent on-shore breeze made much of that very personal, almost stylised, penchant for luxuriant feathery hats which has become almost legendary (opposite page, bottom left). Two more variations on the blue theme were seen in April 1980 when (right) she visited a convalescent home in Leatherhead and attended the thanksgiving service at the City Temple London for the 80th anniversary of the National Free Church Women's Council (far right and opposite page, top left).

and the unfortunate matter of Jeremy Fry who stepped down as best man when details of an eight-year-old criminal conviction engendered covert media pressure. Nevertheless, the Queen Mother realising that her daughter must in all reasonable circumstances be allowed to marry the man of her choice, fully backed the union – this was stated in the official announcement of their engagement and confirmed by the use of Clarence House and Royal Lodge Windsor as the venues for official photographs and camera calls – and when she accompanied the couple to their first official engagement at Covent Garden in March 1960 she beamed with pride as they received the tumultuous approbation of the audience. The marriage two months later lacked nothing in splendour, and the Queen Mother's overwhelmed features as she took her place in Westminster Abbey only strengthened the view that, pleased as she was to see her second daughter happily married, her family instincts were dealt another sad blow as the last of the three people whose lives she had shared for almost forty years spread her wings to make her own life away from home.

"My only wish," the Queen Mother had said in February

The Queen Mother wearing two of her favourite tiaras in recent years. (Right) arriving at the London Palladium in November 1980 for the Royal Variety Performance, where she met the infamous "J.R." (below), Sammy Davis Jnr., and Arthur Askey (bottom) among many others. (Far right) being welcomed by the Prime Minister, Margaret Thatcher, for dinner at No. 10 Downing Street the same month. More evenings out (opposite page): a reception at the Japanese Embassy (bottom left) during Emperor Hirohito's visit in 1971; a visit to the Royal Opera House to see Mayerling *in February 1978 (top left); meeting the stars at the Royal Film Performance in March 1981 (right).*

1952 after her husband's funeral, "is that now I may be allowed to continue the work which we sought to do together." No-one can accuse her of withdrawal symptoms on the scale, for instance, of Queen Victoria after 1861, nor of failing to make full use of the opportunities which offered themselves, almost from the days of her bereavement, to add her own dimension to the functions of the monarch and her family. Like most subsidiary roles in the Royal Family, it was impossible to define but has proved fun to develop. The visit to Rhodesia, which was her first overseas journey since her daughter's Accession, was followed at the rate of

approximately one a year up to 1967 by visits to Canada, North Africa, Australia, New Zealand, the West Indies, East Africa, France, West Germany, Italy and the USA. When she visited the States in 1954, she almost caused a stampede during a shopping expedition in Fifth Avenue, and everywhere she delighted the crowds as effectively as she had in 1939. Then, Eleanor Roosevelt had commended her as "perfect as a Queen, gracious, informed, saying the right thing, and kind." Now as Queen Mother she subdued the most cynical with her immense natural charm. "We cheered the Queen Mother heartily," wrote Labour MP John McGovern, who happened to be there at the time. "I completely lost my proletarian snobbery." Echoes of Harold Nicolson who, in 1939, admitted after watching her in a procession, "we returned to the House with lumps in our throats."

Birthday portraits for the Queen Mother which accentuate her love of gardens and flowers. She was almost lost in a profusion of pink blooms, chosen by Cecil Beaton as the backdrop for her 70th birthday portrait (top right) at Royal Lodge. Its grounds were also chosen for the two photographs (above) by Norman Parkinson to celebrate her 80th birthday. (Top left) the Queen Mother at Clarence House on her 75th birthday, and (opposite) wearing a fresh salad-green outfit two years later.

Many of her visits abroad, particularly in the last decade or so, have been private or concerned mainly with her association with organisations requiring her presence. She has for instance visited Canada seven times since her widowhood, frequently attending ceremonies connected with her Colonelcies-in-Chief of the Black Watch (Royal Highland Regiment) of Canada and the Toronto Scottish Regiment, while her occasional visits to West Germany reveal the importance she attaches to some of the 25 or so regiments and military organisations in which she holds honorary rank.

the Queen Mother began to travel more often than not by air on these long journeys abroad – a reflection of her forward-looking approach to life. She had first taken to flying in July 1935, when she joined her husband for a flight from Hendon to Brussels, but that was nothing to her zestful approach to this now increasingly popular and highly developed form of transport in the early 1950s. In 1952, on a visit to an RAF station, she was taken up in the new Comet aircraft and actually took over the controls. With or without permission, she increased the speed of the engine to almost

There was a reduced royal contingent at the Badminton Horse Trials in April 1982, with the Queen and Prince Philip in Canada, the Prince and Princess of Wales preparing for their Scillies holiday, and Prince Andrew sailing towards the South Atlantic. But the Queen Mother was there as usual, escorted round part of the enormous Badminton estate by the Duke of Beaufort (above).

Her half dozen visits to France since 1956 have almost invariably carried a degree of official status, but she likes to spend a few private days in Paris, the Loire Valley or in the Bordeaux region, where the families of many of the friends she made in her teens and early twenties still live.

By contrast with the sedate royal progresses of the pre-war era,

the limits of its power of retaining stability. That was at 40,000 feet, and she gleefully sent a telegram afterwards to 600 (City of London) Squadron of which she was Home Air Commodore, "Today I took over as first pilot." Her account of the flight sounded confidently cheerful, but Sir Miles Thomas, who was with her at the time, confessed years later that he still shuddered at the thought of that terrifying day.

She was the first member of the Royal Family to travel round the world by air when, in 1958, she visited Australasia, though her return home was several times delayed by successive engine failures. She also followed Prince Philip's early example of using helicopters for short hops across the country between engagements, cutting down considerably on time if not on the cost of fuel. Strictly, because the royal helicopters are part of the Queen's Flight, she has to ask her daughter for permission to use them. There is, of course,

the months of heavy commitments but barring accidents, those schedules have always been scrupulously attended to. "Work," she is said to have drummed into her two daughters during their childhood, "is the rent you pay for life," and even now she tries to eke out her hundred or so public engagements per year to favour as many as possible of the three hundred organisations who rely on her patronage. It takes no mathematician to appreciate that this is no easy task, particularly as the Queen Mother, despite her dislike of anniversaries and undue respect

for precedent, likes to be seen to be especially associated with specific annual events. January will for instance see her taking tea with the ladies of the Women's Institute at West Newton near Sandringham – indeed she often helps to prepare the food, especially if the Queen and Princess Margaret are with her, and rarely comes away without having bought the odd trinket or piece of embroidery worked by one of its members. In February she will attend the King's Lynn Festival of Music and Arts, and in March she revels in the quaint old ceremony of distributing the

no real difficulty, and unlike the Queen, who has travelled by helicopter only once – and that at the behest of security officers during her Silver Jubilee visit to Northern Ireland – the Queen Mother enjoys flying, has never been air-sick, and has made the helicopter part of her everyday life for almost a quarter of a century. She still uses them despite a startling incident in June 1982, when the helicopter she was travelling in from Windsor to Kent had to make an emergency landing owing to suspected engine failure. Although, now in her eighties, the Queen Mother keeps a lighter engagement book than previously, her years of widowhood have never wilfully been devoid of a programme of official duty. Holidays have, as is the royal wont, been sufficiently lengthy to sustain her through

shamrocks to the Irish Guards on St Patrick's Day, wherever one of their battalions may be stationed. This is good fun as much as anything – "One for you – and one for me" ran one recent headline showing the Queen Mother and the battalion commanding officer merrily pinning clumps of shamrock on each other in mutual admiration. April invariably sees the Queen Mother enjoying the country air at the Duke of Beaufort's

visits provide a reminder of the five wonderful years Queen Mary spent there during the war, when she formed such close and informal ties with the staff and local people. "I *have* enjoyed myself here," she said on leaving in 1945. "Here I've been anybody to everybody, and now I shall have to start being Queen Mary all over again!"

The Queen Mother's habitual May engagement is, predictably, the Chelsea Flower Show, one of

the many expressions of her passionate interest in and knowledge of flowers and gardens. Another such annual example comes usually in June when, as long-standing Patron of the London Gardens Society, she spends an afternoon being escorted around the gardens of ordinary folk in Greater London, whose efforts over the past year have won prizes in the Society's annual competition. This is a pleasantly relaxed and relaxing

Badminton estate in Gloucestershire. She has attended almost every year's three-day eventing tournament since its inception in 1949, and the Beauforts – the Duchess is a niece of Queen Mary – play host to her for four days, as they do in March when she stays there in order to attend the Cheltenham race festival each year. Those

Norman Parkinson's original 80th birthday portrait of the Queen Mother – seen (opposite page) with the Queen at Royal Lodge in June 1980 – placed her in as modernistic a setting as some younger members of her family. He also photographed Princess Anne (above left) and her son (right) at Gatcombe Park that summer. Lord Snowdon took the remaining photographs: Lady Diana Spencer at Highgrove House (far right) and at Buckingham Palace (bottom right) in March 1981, Lady Helen Windsor's coming-of-age portraits in April 1982, and the Princess of Wales' 21st birthday study.

engagement, with the Queen Mother talking knowledgeably about her favourite subject, the skills of which – despite now being a "second hand" gardener – she learned from her mother. The horticultural world's greatest tribute to her – the Elizabeth of Glamis rose, developed by Sam McGready – evidences her interest and their appreciation. In this she compares well with the Queen, who has admitted that "I am not particularly renowned for my green fingers."

Queen Elizabeth has attended all the major weddings which now form part of our Royal Family's recent history. Attendants perpetuate the family connections: Princess Anne was bridesmaid to Princess Margaret in May 1960 (right); Lady Sarah Armstrong-Jones attended both Princess Anne in November 1973 (bottom right) and the Princess of Wales in July 1981 (below). Periodic gatherings of the royal clan (opposite page) allow the gradual changes to be marked for posterity.

In June or July the Queen Mother goes on tour of her own five ports – the Cinque Ports on the south-east coast of England, of which she became the 160th Lord Warden, succeeding the late Sir Robert Menzies, in 1978. This ancient office, stemming from the days when the ports constituted Britain's first line of defence in the event of invasion, is coupled with that of Constable of Dover Castle, and

it was on a wet, windy August day in 1979 that she went to Dover to be installed. There was a special hallowing service at the Church of St Mary in Castro, within the Castle precincts, then a stately carriage drive in – appropriately enough – the Scottish State Coach with Prince Edward, Viscount Linley and Lady Sarah Armstrong-Jones into the town. Here, in a candy-striped marquee in the grounds

of Dover College she assumed office, gravely promising to maintain its traditions and obligations, yet twinkling with humour as she referred to the break of tradition which had resulted in her appointment as the first woman to hold it, and again at the thought that she might have to pay for the disposal and burial of any whales washed up on the port's beaches – "a troublesome rider," she thought, to all the traditional privileges. She has visited the ports annually ever since, attending all sorts of formalities from the launching of boats to the Hastings winkle ceremony!

In early September the Queen Mother renews her acquaintance with the people of Braemar at the annual Gathering – a custom which she has faithfully kept up since her marriage. Since Queen Victoria first presided over the Gathering and games in the 1840s, the Royal Family has shown up there in force, and the Queen Mother can almost claim to be the connection between Queen Victoria's first attendance and the patronage offered today by Queen Elizabeth II. November is the month for many anniversaries, not least of which are the Remembrance ceremonies. Like most members

of her family, she attends the Festival of Remembrance at the Royal Albert Hall while on Remembrance Sunday, as her wreath in memory of the fallen is placed for her by her friend and Comptroller Sir Ralph Anstruther, and no doubt remembering the members of her own family who died in two world wars, she watches from a balcony in Whitehall, accompanied by her husband's cousin King Olav V of Norway who attends the ceremony with meticulous regularity as a gesture of thanks for Britain's hospitality to him and his father during their exile. November is

Prominent as ever on the Royal Family's big day out at Epsom, the Queen Mother takes her usual expert interest in the Derby, along with the Queen (right), Prince Philip (far right), Princess Anne (above), the Duke of Gloucester (centre left), Princess Michael of Kent (opposite page, top left), and the Ogilvys (above right). Although the Queen Mother runs horses only in National Hunt races, she shares the Queen's enthusiasm for the Flat.

also the month when the Queen Mother visits the Royal College of Music of which she has for many years been Patron, and frequently attends the annual St Cecilia's Day concert. Every other year, on average, she is the guest of honour at the Royal Variety Performance in London in aid of the Variety Artistes' Benevolent Fund; she usually takes other members of the family with her – either Princess Margaret, or the Duke and Duchess of Kent, or Princess Alexandra and her husband. In November 1980, for a performance in celebration of her 80th birthday, she was

accompanied by her admiring grandson Prince Charles. It has long been the practice, and will presumably remain so, that personal relationships between members of the Royal Family are matters of close secrecy. Prince Charles however has never been one to keep his own counsel where public appreciation of his grandmother is concerned. The death, when he was only three, of the grandfather he will no doubt successfully emulate as King, left a gap in his upbringing which was filled partly by the experienced and sage Lord Mountbatten and partly by the Queen Mother herself. It was she who looked after him in those perplexing years when, as a toddler, he frequently missed his parents as they travelled both

Princess Anne, the first of the Queen Mother's grandchildren to marry, now has two children of whom Peter, seen (below right) with his parents in 1980, has been at school for over a year. Prince Charles' engagement was concluded the following February (below left) while the initiation of Prince Andrew (left) into manhood took him to the Falklands in 1982. Prince Edward (far left) quit Gordonstoun that July for New Zealand, and then Cambridge, while Viscount Linley (right) graduated from woodcraft school to start his own workshop.

in this country and abroad – Princess Elizabeth on official royal duty and the Duke of Edinburgh on naval service until 1950. On a later parental absence, during the Queen's Commonwealth Tour of 1953/4 it is said that the Queen Mother tried to instil a love of gardening in him by providing him with a set of miniature gardening tools which her own daughters had used as children. And it was with his grandmother that he and Princess Anne went to

Portsmouth on the first leg of their journey to Gibraltar to meet his parents on their return. Though the gardening experiment failed, the Queen Mother had better luck with the arts. She is reckoned a woman of middle-brow tastes, perhaps because, as in most walks of life, she insists that any experience should be essentially enjoyable. While she let slip no opportunity to take Prince Charles, in his schoolboy years, to the King's Lynn Festival and

later to Covent Garden and the Royal Opera House, he does remember, with some regret, "being excruciatingly bored by some of it." But, he continued, "my grandmother was one of the chief influences in the sense that she always made everything such fun. She always made those expeditions exciting and enjoyable." He speaks with humility about the debt he owes to that "sparkling, fascinating lady . . . a wonderful example of fun, laughter, warmth, infinite

security and above all such exquisite taste in so many things, (whose) greatest gift is to enhance life for others through her own effervescent enthusiasm for life." She is, he was proud to acknowledge in a foreword to an earlier biography, "one of those extraordinarily rare people who can turn everything into gold." Few impressions of the Queen Mother's matriarchal pride in her grandson are more lasting than her broad, gratified smile as he walked in procession at

The Queen Mother and her daughters pose (left) for 80th birthday pictures by Norman Parkinson, wearing identical blue capes. Deep blue, too, for Princess Anne (below), her regal features framed in diffused light. The Princess of Wales looks less distant (bottom picture) in Snowdon's 21st birthday photograph, while his portrait of Lady Helen Windsor, the only daughter of the Duke and Duchess of Kent, romanticises her coming-of-age (below left) with classic adult finery.

The Queen Mother and relatives at Badminton, April 1982. Youngest grandson Prince Edward escorted her to Badminton church on the final day (below) while the Duchess of Beaufort emerged with the Queen Mother after the service (right).

Caernarvon Castle after his Investiture in 1969 as a wash of applause swelled round its ruined walls, or the almost frail look of endearment, mingled with a perky curiosity, as he exchanged marriage vows with Lady Diana Spencer on that memorable July day in 1981. Prince Charles is not of course the only beneficiary of the Queen Mother's affections for and interest in her growing family. She was overjoyed when Prince Andrew was born in 1960, bending traditional royal

(Overleaf) special cheers greeted the Queen Mother at the wedding of the Prince and Princess of Wales at St Paul's Cathedral in 1981. Escorted by Prince Edward to the service, and by Prince Andrew for the return journey, she looked thrilled with the splendour and pageantry of it all. As the bride and groom walked down the aisle a broad beam of delight lit up her face, though she had dabbed away the occasional tear during the more solemn moments of the marriage service.

silence on personal matters by telling reporters, "He's a lovely little boy" as she attended official engagements the following day. And, not for the last time in celebration of a birthday, she held the five-month-old Prince in her lap as the cameras clicked away on her

sixtieth birthday that August: Prince Charles and Princess Anne had been delegated with the task of taking him from Buckingham Palace to Clarence House for the occasion. Three years later she commissioned the sculptor Belsky to fashion a portrait head of Prince Andrew –

"before he loses that look of babyhood," she was said to have explained. She took him to watch Trooping the Colour in the later 1960s and has indeed continued to accompany the younger members of the family on that annual occasion ever since. In 1975, perhaps in order

to halt the widespread belief that Prince Charles was her favourite grandson, she had one of her 75th birthday portraits taken with Prince Andrew on one side of her and Prince Charles on the other.

In 1981, Prince Andrew accompanied her on the journey

back from St Paul's Cathedral to Buckingham Palace after Prince Charles' wedding, an occasion to which she had been taken in the company of her fourth grandson, Prince Edward. He shares the Queen Mother's love of the outdoor life, as evidenced by his recent attendances at Badminton. Princess Anne has for many years been a regular competitor there, an achievement which she probably

Royal Ascot is another of the Queen Mother's annual magnets, and while she is no fashion extrovert, she enjoys the opportunity to wear some of her colourful summery outfits. The daily order of royal processions changes as different members of her family join the festival: (this page) with the Queen in 1982; (opposite page) with the Queen and Lady Diana Spencer in 1981, and with Princess Margaret in 1982.

There is nothing artificial about the Queen Mother's rapport with her grandchildren, nor is it a merely parochial quality. That, as one of her acquaintances said, "she is especially interested in the young and has a great understanding of them" is evidenced time and time again in many news photographs of her with young people. Her visits to boys' clubs in some of the tougher areas of London are famous, and although she could not play snooker to save her life, she will take a game, though strangely left-handed, pot at a cluster of snooker balls as a token of her goodwill on such visits. On other occasions she seems to have shown great interest in the heavy tattoos on the arm of a "rocker" in south east London, and in the metal-studded leather wrist-bands

owes largely to the efforts of the Queen Mother, who in 1968 took her to a cellar party in the City of London in honour of the British Equestrian team which had returned as triumphant gold medallists from the Olympic Games in Mexico. "As a beginner at eventing, I was overawed," the Princess confessed, but the experience clearly spurred her on to greater things. When she married Captain Mark Phillips in 1973, the Queen Mother gave her an aquamarine and diamond tiara for her wedding present and, for the wedding ceremony itself, loaned a tiara that she had previously lent Princess Elizabeth for her wedding in 1947.

worn by another rock fan at London dock recently, when she visited an Operation Drake enterprise for unemployed youngsters. "I'd been told she was a bit of a fascist," he said afterwards, "but I think she's

1960 the journalist Godfrey Winn paid tribute to her on the eve of her sixtieth birthday with an article entitled, "She's sixty tomorrow and if you think she smiles too easily . . ." It contained a sad catalogue of the

alright – a nice lady."
It may have seemed unjust that this "nice lady" was obliged to wait for almost sixty years before she could sit back and enjoy life to the full again. As it happened, it would have been due to her as a commoner on reaching normal retiring age, and indeed the rewards have since been great, but by the middle of the 1950s she must have felt that Fate had only rarely offered her the benefit of unspoiled happiness to compensate for the successive anxieties of her life. More, there were surely times when she regretted, in principle at least, her eventual agreement to become the wife of a member of the Royal Family. In August

tribulations which had beset her in the previous quarter of a century, and a litany of complaints about the injustice of it all.
It is doubtful if anyone would have blamed her for calling it a day at that point and fading into retirement, but that has clearly not been her way. Perhaps

The wedding of Mr Nicholas Soames, grandson of Sir Winston Churchill, to Miss Catherine Weatherall provided another opportunity for a family outing. The Queen Mother took Princess Margaret, the Prince of Wales and Lady Diana Spencer to the service, held at St Margaret's Church Westminster in May 1981.

mindful of Queen Mary's indignation when, after a reign of almost sixty years, Queen Wilhelmina of the Netherlands abdicated the Dutch throne in 1948 – "Wilhelmina is 68," she wrote, "and that is no age to retire" – the Queen Mother sailed on to the eventual serenity which the last two and a half decades have produced. Her years as grandmother of a growing family have been characterised by the judicious combination of business and pleasure.

One of her main pleasures has undoubtedly been her interest in and support for horse-racing. It began when she was still unmarried, but increased considerably when as King, her husband took over the responsibility for the Royal Stud which King George V had nurtured during his long reign. One of the old King's horses, Feola, bought in 1934 for only three thousand guineas, foaled for his son and daughter-in-law a regular procession of winning offspring including Hypericum, which won the One Thousand Guineas in 1946, and Angelola, winner of the Yorkshire Oaks. From Angelola's successive coverings, the present Queen benefitted in the early years of

– she seems never to have ridden a horse during adulthood – but in the cautious way of a propective owner. She persuaded Princess Elizabeth to come in with her, and they bought in joint names their first jumper, Monaveen, which trainer Peter Cazalet purchased on their behalf for a thousand guineas. Monaveen was an instant success, winning four races and coming fifth in the Grand National, and his royal owners were delighted with this first flush of triumph. Unfortunately the horse broke a leg later and had to be destroyed; Princess Elizabeth lost her enthusiasm almost immediately, and left her mother, who was by now quite won over to the sport, to have another try. She did, and

her reign from prestigious victories on the Flat, but by then the Queen Mother had wandered off to pastures new. In 1949 Lord Mildmay of Flete, speaking with her at a house party during Ascot week, entranced her with his stories of the excitement and dangers of National Hunt racing, and it was not long before she herself had decided to branch out and try her luck at racing over the sticks. Not personally of course

with her next purchase – Manicou, formerly owned by Lord Mildmay, who tragically drowned the same year – there were cheers for royal victories in 1950.

It seemed at that point that hurdling and steeple-chasing would be Queen Elizabeth's new and lasting passion and, after lack-lustre fortunes on the track

The Queen Mother paid a visit to Canada House in London to open its new cultural centre in February 1982. This official engagement would have brought back personal memories: it was her last before the thirtieth anniversary of the death of her husband, with whom she carried out a successful, extremely popular six week visit to Canada in 1939.

brought her the reward of three hundred winners.

Like all successful racing stories, hers was not without its tragedies, but mercifully there are few to recount. The one which makes all others pale into insignificance is, of course, the sad tale of Devon Loch in 1956, the Queen's best ever Grand National prospect who, having cleared the last of three dozen fences well in the lead, collapsed on the run in. His legs gave way and splayed out flat, leaving him – it seemed in that split-second – to bounce horribly on his belly while other horses of less stamina than he galloped past to take the honours. A dramatic series of photographs exists showing the stages of collapse, but close scrutiny has never revealed a satisfactory explanation, and his jockey Dick Francis could only put it down

in the next three seasons, this has indeed proved to be the case. With the renewed efforts of Peter Cazalet and the full support of his royal patron, the Queen Mother began to redeem her luck in the mid 1950s, when a long period of fine and

consistent successes began. By 1964 she had been credited with her hundredth win; by 1970 her two hundredth; she saw no fewer than fifty winners home in the following two seasons, and by the end of the decade her thirty-year-old involvement

to the massive swell of cheers which unnerved Devon Loch as the Queen Mother's first National win was about to be chalked up. Another photograph at the very point of the collapse shows the Royal Stand packed with members of the Queen Mother's family, her friends, and associates in the racing fraternity, with varying expressions on their faces demonstrating that some had just realised the nature and extent of the tragedy while others quite clearly had not. It is the perfect illustration of the maxim "Many a slip 'twixt cup and lip," as true in racing as in

any other walk of life.

"Well, that's racing," was the Queen Mother's only immediate comment as she went down to the winner's enclosure to congratulate the owners of ESB, the winning horse, themselves full of embarrassment at this quirkish accident which had taken the prospective prize almost from the Queen Mother's very hands and turned it over to them. But, not surprisingly, there were no recriminations. "She never turned a hair," said the Duke of Devonshire. "It was the most perfect display of dignity that I have ever witnessed. I hope," he added, knowing that a Russian delegation was positioned in a nearby box, "that the Russians saw it." The Queen Mother's thoughts then turned to the jockey and stable lads, all of whom were in tears. "I must go down and comfort those poor people," she said, and spent the rest of the available time commiserating with them and the trainer, who like her were deeply stunned by the experience of having, as she later put it, "success snatched from one, even at the last fence." She has owned a few really game and top class chasers, such as The Rip and Laffy, as well as the occasional long-

serving horses like Gay Record, whom she bought for 250 guineas and who raced for eleven years, winning nine and being placed in almost two dozen of his fifty-nine races. In 1964, the year of her hundredth winner, she topped the winning owners' list with prize money of over £9,000. The 25th anniversary of her adventure into the sport was crowned, in the 1974/75 season, by an accumulated total of £100,000 in winnings, and although her successes have in more recent years been harder to come by – Master Andrew and Cranbourne Towers are the current mainstays

of her achievements – she is still bringing up young prospects of four and five years old as an act of faith in a future which she believes is always worth fighting for.

The origins of her involvement may be in the genes: John Bowes won the Derby four times; the thirteenth Earl of Strathmore, the Queen Mother's grandfather, was a famous, if not a brilliantly successful owner, as was the Portland family from whom her mother was descended. And it is in the Strathmore colours – blue shirt and sleeves with buff stripes, and gold and black cap – that her jockeys ride for her today. The Queen Mother is no mere fireside enthusiast, although it is well known that when her official engagements prevent her from attending race meetings, she will watch what she can on television, and keep in contact with the course by means of the

"blower" – a telephonic system more frequently associated with bookmakers and betting shops to keep them abreast of up-to-the-minute on-course developments. But attendances at race meetings close to London – Sandown Park, Plumpton and Windsor for instance – are almost *de rigueur,* as is her annual pilgrimage to Cheltenham for the three-day race festival which is widely regarded as the Royal Ascot of steeplechasing, with its Gold Cup Day and the Queen Mother two-mile Champion Hurdle. When she attends any meeting, there is surprisingly little fuss:

are bespattered with mud. I once saw her deep in conference with her "team" over the performance of her horse which had just come in second, and it was evident to the crowd that there was some kind of dispute. Eventually, her voice rang out, "Well, *I* think he ran a *marvellous* race," and off she toddled back to the grandstand, leaving the others unconvinced, yet in no doubt of the strength of her appreciation.

She is of course equally interested, though less personally involved, in the Flat, and her annual attendances at the high social holidays of

one is merely suddenly aware of a couple of policemen gently clearing a path for her as she moves from the grandstand to the paddock or to the winner's enclosures, and the crowds reform immediately she has passed. And in those enclosures she will chat knowledgeably with her trainer – Fulke Walwyn succeeded Cazalet in 1973 – and discuss the race with her jockey no matter how much his features

Britain and the Commonwealth paid enthusiastic tributes to the Queen Mother amid celebrations to mark her 80th birthday. On 15th July 1980, some three weeks in advance, London was the scene of colourful processions as the Royal Family, including Princess Alice and the Duchess of Gloucester (far left), Princess Anne, Princess Margaret, Lady Sarah Armstrong-Jones (above left), and the Queen, Prince Philip and Prince Edward (above) attended a thanksgiving service in St Paul's Cathedral. The Archbishop of Canterbury delivered a moving and appreciative address ending with the words "Thank you, Your Majesty. Thanks be to God." Crowds swarmed round Buckingham Palace to acclaim the Queen Mother when she appeared on its balcony afterwards.

Epsom on Derby Day and Royal Ascot give the public the opportunity to see her and her family studying the form – particularly at Epsom – as they stand at the side of the course watching the runners canter by. It is on these occasions that, with her relatives, she really lets herself go, pointing, waving and clapping for all to see as the racing reaches its peaks of excitement.

At the other end of the spectrum of her interests is her love of the arts. We have already

opportunity to meet artistes after a performance – a practice which she had assimilated certainly as early as 1943 when, at a poetry reading recital in aid of the Free French at London's Aeolian Hall, she invited all the participating poets to meet her in an ante-room during the interval. (She is incidentally a great reader of poems and one poet, probably apocryphally, has related that she used to sit up in bed reading poetry, with a large box of chocolates by her side.) Nowadays it is after the great

seen how she has influenced the Prince of Wales' own appreciation of certain art forms to the point where he perhaps can be compared with his aunt Princess Margaret in his love of musical and theatrical excellence, and her own following has been prolonged and extensive. She enjoys the

London shows that she is seen mingling with a wide range of performers – whether it is the great Italian tenor Pavarotti at the Royal Albert Hall or the minor stars of television after the Royal Variety Performance in London's West End. And if that meeting with the stars takes place on the stage, as it often

does, you can hear a pin drop as the audience strains, usually in vain, to catch just a few syllables of the royal conversation.

The Queen Mother has had many tributes paid to her by representatives from the world of the arts. The composer Eric Coates, composing a suite of music in celebration of the

Queen's Coronation in 1953, called it *The Three Elizabeths,* the middle section *Elizabeth of Glamis* was a tribute to the Queen Mother. At the other extreme she was possibly surprised, certainly delighted, when at the end of a Royal Variety Performance some twenty years ago Maurice

almost pessimistic paintings show the Castle surrounded, as if allegorically, by the foreboding clouds of a terrible war. As we now know, Windsor Castle survived the war intact and, as the Queen Mother endearingly says, "Now we have the Pipers and the Castle!" Her other contribution – in the opposite direction as it were – to the arts has been her unfailing patience with portrait painters and her understanding of their requirements. Augustus John said that she was "angelic,

Less formal, but equally loyal and sincere congratulations surrounded the Queen Mother when, on 4th August 1980 she made her annual public appearance outside Clarence House to receive tributes from the Household Brigades (left) and vocal greetings from the crowds.

posing so often and with such cheerfulness." He was never an easy man to please, and on one occasion refused to paint her portrait unless, having arrived at the Palace sober, he would be permitted to leave it drunk. So she arranged for a bottle of sherry and a bottle of brandy to be placed in a cupboard in the room in which he was working, so that he could have recourse to it as he wished. In a later excess of consideration for him, she even had a string quartet playing for him in an adjacent room, but it was evidently not to his taste. When, some time afterwards, she asked him to paint a portrait of Princess Margaret she pleaded, "I could easily bring her to your studio, and I promise I won't bring an orchestra with me." She has occasionally asked for a favour in return: after seeing the finished product of the five sittings she gave to the painter

Chevalier sought permission to dedicate the song "You must have been a beautiful baby" to her.

Although her connoisseurship of the fine arts is not thought to be comprehensive, she has made a significant contribution to the Royal Family's acquisition of paintings. Apart from her own preference for many of the well known modern artists, she had the foresight to commission John Piper to paint views of Windsor Castle at the beginning of the war, in case anything happened to it as the result of enemy action. This was done, and a set of unusually dark,

Richard Stone, she enquired whether he could kindly "take a little off my waist."

Her easy-going and winning approach with portrait-painters, who have historically had to preserve a delicate balance between the demands of artistic integrity and the vanity of their subjects, is the Queen Mother's *forte* – a mere extension of the

Vendors of balloons (bottom) and other souvenirs did a roaring trade as young and old clamoured to offer cards, flowers and gifts to Britain's most popular octogenarian. The Queen Mother's immediate family stood with her at the gates of Clarence House and the Queen and Princess Margaret lent a hand in taking the weight of their mother's unending stream of presents.

gracious yet concerned attitude she adopts with everyone she meets. "It is," said Cecil Beaton, one of her great friends and for many years her favourite photographer, "her empathy and her understanding of human nature that endear her to everyone she talks to; she even makes it seem impossible that people should behave badly or that things could go wrong." Harold Nicolson who had described her in 1936 as "charm personified," said three years later that "she really does manage to convey to each individual in the crowd that he or she have a personal greeting. I think," he added, echoing the thoughts of many others, "it is because of her brilliant blue eyes." He repeated the same sentiments in 1941: "She has that quality of making everybody feel that they and they alone are being spoken to. It is I think because she has very

large eyes which she opens very wide and turns straight upon one." And again in May 1945, he spoke of "a truly miraculous faculty of making each individual feel that it is him whom she has greeted and to him that was devoted that lovely smile." Even by 1958 the magic had not worn off: Nicolson saw her when she opened Morley College that October and praised her "astonishing gift of being sincerely interested in dull people and dull occasions."

It has always of course been open to the cynic to affirm that any lady would quite happily smile her way through life given the enviable circumstances in which the Queen Mother finds herself today, or to wonder whether it is indeed true that, as one of her staff is reported to

A favourite deep-turquoise velvet outfit almost matching the Queen Mother's eyes, was seen frequently in 1982, as in February (above, top right and far left) when she visited St Peter's Church Walworth for a thanksgiving service, and the following month when she opened the Kingston YWCA at Surbiton (left and opposite page).

The Queen Mother's glowing personality was matched by her richly patterned evening dress at a Royal Albert Hall concert in April 1982, at which Luciano Pavarotti made his one and only London appearance that year. The Queen Mother, who shares a love of music with Princess Margaret and Prince Charles, was clearly thrilled by Pavarotti's gallantry as he greeted her after the performance (opposite page, centre).

have said, she has not spoken "a cross word in forty years; there aren't any unlovely foibles in her make-up." Indeed a former Chester Herald of Arms, no less, questioned whether her nature was so invariable as it seemed. In his entertaining though somewhat flippant book *The British Monarchy at Home,* James Frere tells how after her marriage "she soon earned the name of the 'Smiling Duchess'. This was not always applied to her in the kindest way, people averring that it was impossible for her to be so permanently good-natured as she would lead them to believe by her everlasting smile, which must surely be put on for the benefit of the public, and that whenever she got home it fell from her like a mask to be replaced by a perfectly vile temper and the unkindest behaviour to all around her."

This is an hilariously irreverent thought and one that might even appeal to the Queen Mother's humour, but the chances are that it is far wide of the mark. In recent years, when the comings and goings of staff at

Buckingham Palace, Kensington Palace and Gatcombe Park have been matters of almost immediate public knowledge, not a single report of dissention or intolerance at Clarence House has soured the traditionally perfect relationship between the Press and the Queen Mother's household. Indeed the last occasion of any serious threat of impaired relations was in the late 1950s when her name was romantically linked with a 74-year-old member of her household, Sir Arthur Penn, a long-standing friend of the late King and herself. Despite a fair degree of sympathy and popular support for a much-rumoured marriage – "She is too beautiful to be

alone," wrote one newspaper reader – Clarence House denied the speculation as "complete and absolute nonsense." But if Mr. Frere has a point at all, it is that the Queen Mother has realised, earlier and more readily than some of her family, that one of the main obligations of the monarchy is that its members should be seen to be enjoying rather than enduring the programme of duties they undertake. It is nonsense to say, as many have, that the Queen Mother's schedules of engagements are decided for her and that she is left to carry them out as best she may. She, like all other members of her family, decides primarily which she would like, or ought, or feels

bound to attend, and so there is a presumption that most of her duties will provide a degree of interest and personal enjoyment. Where the Queen Mother scores is in allowing that enjoyment to shine through, sometimes gently, sometimes positively ebulliently, but always with transparent clarity. One observer commented that she laid a foundation stone and made a speech as though it was the most exciting way of spending an afternoon that she could imagine.

The secret of course lies in the essential quality for any person regularly seen in public, and from whom much is always expected – showmanship. It may be disrespectful, even *lèse-majesté,* to talk of the Royal Family's existence as a parade of superstars in a never-ending series of highly-orchestrated

are qualities which lent themselves admirably to Beaton's own classic official photographs which he took of the Queen Mother back in the late 1930s, but her smile is not really the "impervious public facade" which it has been accused of being. "It is," she told Beaton in 1939, "so hard to know when *not* to smile." Eleanor Roosevelt, in one of her few reservations about the Queen Mother, thought that "she was a little self-consciously regal" in 1939, but if there was a deliberate pose, it was almost certainly one which the American public expected, and which Her Majesty knew they expected, "This one's always a hit," said another American in

public appearances, but however serious the occasion to which they are obliged to lend their presence, there are a million eyes watching for almost every gesture and reaction as if the future of the world depended upon it. The Queen Mother has perfected that quality – obviously to the point where Mr. Frere suspects its sincerity – but to the evident satisfaction of a

nation whose admiration for her now verges on the reverential. "Of course," said Cecil Beaton, "there is something of the great actress about her, and in public she has to put on a show that never fails. It is her special ability to be touching and wistful with a simple and beautiful grace, to use gestures which are really unhurried. Her Majesty moves in slow motion." These

1954, using the language of stardom with which British royalty is often blessed in the States, and the radio and news journalist Godfrey Talbot has confirmed that "she thrives on public scrutiny." A less appreciative remark came from the pen of the republican Willie Hamilton MP who, as a prelude to one of his many scathing attacks on the Queen Mother's Civil List allowance, opined that "if a personal public image is the thing to cultivate today, then the Queen Mother is the best of gardeners." Neatly put, but clearly you can't please them all. The Canadians were pleased to see her in 1939 when, we are

even the most *blasé* débutantes must have been impressed when, in 1951, she revived the old pre-war custom by which they were presented individually to the sovereign, because she guessed that they would like to feel they had personally met their host and hostess.
But surely the most popular illustration of the Queen Mother's willingness to "go on public display" is the annual (or almost annual) appearance she makes, and has made since her seventieth birthday, on the narrow, flower-bedecked balcony of Clarence House, to acknowledge the cheers and good wishes of a crowd, now

told, she got out of bed during a journey on the blue and silver train, put on her dressing gown and a tiara, and waved from the observation platform to a crowd of well wishers who had waited through the night to see her; Zulus were equally delighted that on a boiling hot day in 1947 she insisted on dressing in full formal evening gown with tiara and jewels because "this is how they would expect me to look, and they'd know it was me;"

growing larger by the year, who wait for much of the morning of 4th August to wish her Happy Birthday. Her appearance is usually only brief, though a few years ago it was extended to include a walk to the house's outer gate where the sight of small children thrusting flowers and presents into her hands is now familiar. The practice is now so well established – she has failed to appear only once recently, and that was in the

Mid-May 1982 found the Queen Mother in Paris, visiting France once again as she has, on and off, since her teens. This particular visit was part private, part official, the main official purpose being to open a new wing of the Hertford British Hospital, of which she is Patron, on 12th May – the 45th anniversary of her Coronation. That afternoon, she took tea with President Mitterrand who accompanied Her Majesty to the main entrance of the Elysée Palace (these pages) for her departure. Having visited France officially five times in the previous quarter of a century, and on many other private occasions, the Queen Mother knows the Bordeaux region, and the Chateaux of the Loire well. It is said that she influenced the decision to send Princess Anne for a stay in France in the early 1960s.

wake of the Prince and Princess of Wales' wedding just six days before her 81st birthday – that it is the only thing which keeps her from beginning her summer holiday first at Sandringham, where her husband was born and died, and then in Scotland. Part of that aptitude for the very public side of her existence is reflected in the Queen Mother's clothes, something for which, like all other elements of her public appearance, she is more than prepared to make time. Despite the death a few years ago of Norman Hartnell, (he used, incidentally, to send her red roses every birthday – the

number according to her age – but he stopped increasing the size of the bouquet after she reached six dozen years!) the Queen Mother still looks to his London fashion house for most of her day clothes. Although in the highly fashion-conscious days before the last war she was a sophisticated dresser – "I have never seen her looking so beautiful," wrote Chips Channon in 1939. "She was dressed to perfection" – she has always avoided any risk of artificiality without losing the essential elegance on formal or semi-formal occasions. Her style has for many years been distinctive

rather then exciting, safe rather than adventurous – "Why should I not be known for my style of dressing?" she recently asked. But, with her straightish lines and the pastel or light colours which, she feels, make it easier for the public to pick her out, she always looks becoming. She prefers not to wear thick, heavy clothes except for the occasional raw day at Badminton or the races; she adores pure silk when it is appropriate, and persists, with unquestionable success, in wearing upon her petite, still dainty feet those small high-heeled shoes and slingbacks

181

which help to raise her an inch or two above her natural height of five feet two inches.

Her clothes are designed as a result of private fittings and discussions at Clarence House, where a Hartnell advisor, along with a tailor and dressmaker, spend about an hour each fortnight thumbing through pattern books and pads of materials. The Queen Mother makes her own decisions, based on the suggestions of her visitors, and what gratifies them most is that "although she has had thousands of outfits in her time she always shows undiminished interest in the one you are making." Although many of her clothes are of turquoise or aquamarine, she is not keen on wearing green which she considers unlucky. King George VI never liked it, and she hardly ever wore it again after his death.

The Queen Mother on her 60th birthday with grandson Prince Andrew (left). Her 82nd birthday saw the christening of Prince William, whose first official pictures (bottom and opposite) were released the previous week. (Below) Princess Anne and son Peter, in 1978.

Superstition does not play a large part in the Queen Mother's make-up, but she is evidently wary of the number thirteen. The story goes that when Princess Margaret's birth came to be registered at Glamis, the next number on the register was thirteen. Her mother therefore decided to wait until, eventually, a Mrs. Gevina Brown came to register her son George, who was born three days after Princess Margaret. She too was superstitious, but decided to register her baby's birth if it

would help the Duchess of York to proceed with the Princess' registration. And when, as Queen Mother, she rode with Prince Charles to the Thanksgiving Service at St Paul's Cathedral for her eightieth birthday, it was in a carriage, sitting opposite a seat to which had been pinned a horseshoe for good luck. The national celebrations to mark the Queen Mother's 80th

After her annual tour of the Cinque Ports in June 1982 the Queen Mother sailed in the Royal Yacht Britannia *to Portsmouth where she disembarked (top left) to a warm welcome from waiting crowds. A Royal Wedding glass goblet (top) provided a change from the usual bouquets.*

There was a faint hint of mischief even in the Queen Mother's eye (below, far right) when in May 1982 she visited Smithfield Market and became the delighted target of good natured lèse-majesté at the hands of its many Cockney stall-holders. Interspersed among the formalities of her tour of London's most famous meat market, organised to celebrate, of all things, the centenary of the first meat shipment from New Zealand to Britain, were spontaneous acts of gallantry from meat cutters, porters and packers as they seized her hands and kissed them, and serenaded her inspection of the main hall with patriotic songs.

birthday took place on 15th July 1980, three weeks before the actual anniversary. It was a day of the finest weather and London was in a mood of great informal festivity for this unprecedented tribute to a Queen Dowager: there had for example been no comparable occasion for Queen Mary's eightieth birthday in 1947, an anniversary which, according to her official biographer, came as something of a shock. For once, the Queen Mother was the focus of all attention even to the prejudice of her daughter, who willingly ceded to her the privilege of being the last to

There is arguably no subject nearer to the Queen Mother's heart, nor more readily identified with her than that of the garden. Her patronage of the London Gardens Society is now long established, and marked by her annual tours of prize-winning gardens in various parts of the capital. On 14th July 1982 she visited gardens in Kensington (these pages) and Wandsworth, casting an expert eye (top centre) as she wandered through allées, engaging in erudite horticultural conversation with her hosts.

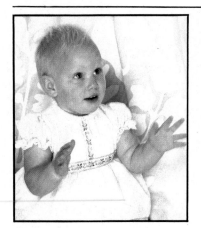

Norman Parkinson's portrait of Queen Elizabeth the Queen Mother (opposite page), taken to mark her 80th birthday, combines the grandeur of formal evening dress with the smile of benign indulgence. Parkinson also took the supremely regal picture of Princess Anne (bottom right) and these delightful photographs of her two children, Peter and Zara. The portfolio was released to celebrate the 34th birthday of Captain Phillips in September 1982, and his son's 5th birthday two months later.

arrive at St Paul's and the first to leave after the service. On the balcony of Buckingham Palace afterwards it was the Queen and Duke of Edinburgh who again made way for the Queen Mother as she emerged three times from the famous French windows to acknowledge the plaudits of a huge mass of wellwishers – tourists, holiday makers or just local office workers more than willing to take the morning off to pay her tribute.

But that was by no means all. Earlier that month she had attended a garden party at the Palace of Holyroodhouse in Edinburgh during the Queen and Prince Philip's traditional week's summer tour of Scotland. They put on a fantastic display of music and formation marching on those huge, lush green grounds, and the Queen Mother met several old friends among the thousand

guests in the course of the three hour party. The following day, detachments of Highland regiments gave their own musical and military tribute, with massed bands performing in a steady drizzle of rain, though that did not stop the crowd from turning up in large numbers to watch. That night, at a reception at Holyroodhouse she danced some Scottish reels – one of her favourite forms of dancing – which she participates in during the Christmas staff dance at Windsor, the Ghillies' Ball at Balmoral each summer and, if she is in Scotland in July, at the Scottish Pipers' Ball in Edinburgh. Indeed it is said that she taught her future sister-in-law Princess Marina of Greece how to dance Scottish reels during one of her visits to Balmoral in 1934.

The day after London celebrated the Queen Mother's 80th birthday, she went to St James's Park to plant a rose bush on a new section of the Rose Walk which had been established in her honour, and the following day she attended another garden party, this time one of the four held that year at Buckingham Palace, especially arranged to entertain representatives from the hundreds of organisations with which she is connected as President, Patron or by honorary rank. Later still that July she paid her annual visit to the Royal Tournament, the organisers of which could not resist weighing in with their tribute. The service units whose titular head she is put on a special display for her, and she stood applauding each event appreciatively from the Royal Box. She was especially pleased to hear a new marching tune

"The Castle of Mey" specially composed for the occasion and played to her for the first time by a Highland regiment.

The climax of the celebrations was the day – 4th August – when she effectively entered her ninth decade. She certainly didn't look it, as she stood by the open gates of her London home overwhelmed by applause and cheers, surrounded by children with presents by the hundredweight and flowers by the dozen – so many indeed that the Queen and Princess Margaret had to come forward and form part of a human chain to relieve her of the unending supply. Behind her were other

members of her family – Prince Charles, Prince Edward, Viscount Linley and Lady Sarah Armstrong-Jones – and before her was a crowd of people who, when they were not standing back to let pass the Household Brigades as they played "Happy Birthday To You," surged forward holding clusters of balloons of all colours – including the silver helium filled affairs which first saw the light of day that year – and bearing messages of good wishes, protestations of love and the familiar appellation "Queen

Mum." It was later revealed that more than two hundred bouquets, many of them roses, and sackfuls of presents had been delivered to Clarence House that day. That night, the Queen and Prince Philip took her, with Prince Charles and Princess Margaret, to the Royal Opera House at Covent Garden to see the Gala première of Sir Frederick Ashton's ballet Rhapsody. Afterwards the company presented her with a huge pink and white birthday cake but, whether out of tact or respect for the royal lungs, crowned it with only a single candle for her to blow out before the ceremonial cutting. "It was the nicest birthday present I've ever had," she told Sir Frederick afterwards.

That day was the climax of the family and national celebrations, though it was also marked by other events throughout the

A subdued celebration for the Queen Mother, seen (opposite page) leaving St Paul's Cathedral with Prince Charles, Princess Anne and their spouses after the service to commemorate the end of hostilities in the Falklands, in July 1982. This was the first public engagement for the Princess of Wales since Prince William's birth a month earlier. Another link with Prince Charles characterised the Queen Mother's visit aboard the Thames sailing barge Dannebrog at St Katharine's Dock in London, also in July. This yacht is the team base of the Operation Drake Fellowship which, inaugurated under Prince Charles' auspices in the 1970s, offers training courses to unemployed school-leavers in Britain's urban areas.

country. The national and local newspapers ran lengthy articles and colour supplements paying tribute to her long years of service, and a commemorative postage stamp, bearing one of Norman Parkinson's 75th birthday portraits of her was issued in Britain. Precedent was again made when a special Crown was minted, bearing the Queen's effigy on the obverse and her mother's portrait, together with the punning arms of bows and lions on the reverse. Several portfolios of official pictures, again by Norman Parkinson, were issued, some of the Queen Mother cosily enjoying a fine June day in the garden of Royal Lodge Windsor, others of her in evening dress and tiara, seen wistfully through paned glass, and most imposing of all a set showing the Queen Mother with her two daughters the Queen and Princess Margaret, all dressed in the same brilliant electric blue capes adorned by the obligatory three row pearl necklaces and diamond brooches. Meanwhile the National Portrait Gallery, in appreciation of the time she has given up to the demands of portrait painters through the years, put on an exhibition of her portraits and photographs since her very earliest childhood, and the Royal Photographic Society mounted an appreciative display under the title "Many Happy Returns" at the new National Centre of Photography, with its excellent facilities, at the Octagon in Bath. Media tributes included a three part radio biography of the Queen Mother's eighty years, a one hundred minute television documentary which took its title "In This Your Honour" from the words of her Coronation Service and in which she commented on the successive lengths of newsreel and film footage by means of a reassuring voice-over technique. The BBC admitted

that this in particular had been a marathon undertaking, but drew comfort from the fact that "It should provide the basis for another tribute on her 90th birthday." At the same time the modern predilection for video films was satisfied by an hour long cassette documentary called "Portrait of a Great Lady." Its presenter and narrator was the actor David Niven who said, "Like many people who shared the decades with her, I feel that in a way she has lived part of our lives for us."

That year, we know, and the opportunity it afforded for ordinary people to express or lend weight to their feelings for her, gave her much pleasure, and the Queen made a special

An informal outdoor royal birthday gathering to which all were welcome: these two youngsters (top) were among the hundreds of people who waited for a glimpse of the Queen Mother outside Clarence House (above) on the morning of her 82nd birthday, just before attending Prince William's christening. Predictably the single marigold was as acceptable as any official bouquet. A single rose, too, (left) for the Queen Mother during her 1982 visit to London Gardens – she is most at home against this typical backdrop of well-tended colourful blooms in natural settings (opposite page).

point of reminding her people of the significance of those celebrations in her Christmas message to the people of the Commonwealth that December. But only two months later the Queen Mother was called upon once again to be of service, when Lady Diana Spencer, engaged at the end of February 1981 to Prince Charles, had to be accommodated at Clarence House during the five months

The christening of Prince William at Buckingham Palace meant more to the Queen Mother than a great family occasion: it focused upon the unsuspecting child born to be the eventual successor to her husband – his great grandfather King George VI. Prince Charles was canny enough to mark a further significance – the link between Prince William's birth and the Victorian era – by choosing the Queen Mother's 82nd birthday (4th August 1982) for the christening.

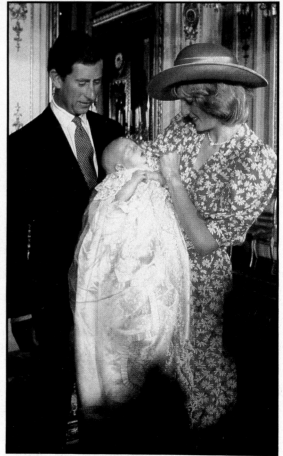

preceding her marriage. This was a particularly pleasing coincidence for the Queen Mother whose closest confidante and lady-in-waiting, Ruth Lady Fermoy, was Lady Diana's grandmother: it was indeed that same lady whose confinement had coincided with King George V's death in 1936. It was thus at Clarence House that after the royal engagement was officially announced Prince Charles and his fiancée joined their respective grandmothers for a celebration dinner, and it was there too that Lady Diana began to learn something of the very different life-style that her recruitment into the Royal Family would bring. Much of the

been through it all nearly sixty years before. She had clearly learnt to be as wily as the Press whose efforts to trace Lady Diana during a long and difficult courtship were effectively thwarted when the Queen Mother allowed her to use Birkhall as a convenient and reasonably private base from which to arrange meetings with the Prince of Wales in Scotland in the summer of 1980. In the wake of the enormous publicity engendered by their wedding in July 1981, the Queen Mother made little of her 81st birthday that August. Her 82nd however more than made up for that. In June 1982, the Princess of Wales had given birth to a

formal protocol was passed on by the Queen's senior lady-in-waiting, Lady Susan Hussey, but there could have been no more sympathetic mentor to understand and advise upon the swift and sometimes strenuous transition to royal status than the Queen Mother herself, who had

A tradition for sixty years is the Royal Family's attendance at the annual Braemar Games. 1982 (these pages) was no less a family occasion than others, with the Princess of Wales enjoying her second visit (above) and the Queen providing some family fun (top) during the presentation of prizes.

healthy baby boy, Prince William, whose reign will, God willing, take the fascinating story of Britain's Royal Family into the second half of the 21st century. It was the most considerate expression of Prince Charles' sense of history and appreciation of all he owes to his grandmother that he should have chosen her 82nd birthday – 4th August 1982 – for the christening of his six week old son. Oddly, and unexpectedly, there was no George or Albert in the child's quartet of names – William Arthur Philip Louis – which were pronounced over him as water from the River Jordan was spooned over him, but the Queen Mother's presence provided the links with the past which Prince Charles was anxious to secure and have recorded. Just as Queen Mary

had held him on her knee in 1948, so Queen Elizabeth the Queen Mother, a visible connection between two vastly different eras, cradled the future King in her lap. Prince William's sense of occasion was not quite as well developed: he had obviously become hungry during the ceremony, and the Queen Mother's only comment as she withstood his vocal assaults on her was, "Well, at least he's got a good pair of lungs."

That evening she visited the Drury Lane Theatre in London to see a performance of Gilbert and Sullivan's "Pirates of Penzance" and, as for her 80th birthday, there was a cake for her to cut. With less consideration than previously, they had mounted 82 candles in the icing, but at least some of

the cast were there to help her blow them out. She did not on this occasion eat any, but slices were distributed amongst the company, and there was rumoured to be a healthy black market for the remaining portions in the following days. The serenity which now graces her days provides a fitting, well deserved postludium to the many years of strain, effort and worry which have accounted for so much of her adult life. In coping with adversity, she has of course strengthened the institution of monarchy immeasurably. Her yearning for quiet domesticity in the early days was hardly gratified when events which she had not foreseen and which she viewed with horror and revulsion overwhelmed her.

The Queen Mother arriving (above) for the Royal Variety Performance at the Theatre Royal, Drury Lane in November 1982. On this occasion she was accompanied by her grand-daughter Lady Sarah Armstrong-Jones, and by her niece Princess Alexandra and the Hon. Angus Ogilvy. (Left and above left) the same month, she paid her annual visit to the Royal College of Music in London – her last engagement before the celebrated fishbone incident which put her in hospital for several days. In December the Queen Mother, following Princess Michael's example the year before, presented awards to 1982's Children of Courage at Westminster Abbey – this was the ninth such ceremony since the awards were first inaugurated.

Amid the transient but vociferous clamour for a Republic in 1936 she, nervously at first but with the growing confidence that mastery of a new job brings, brought the monarchy to a new peak of popularity by her meticulous public support of her husband and by the additional strength which she gave him in private, the extent of which we shall probably never fully appreciate. That popularity was achieved within the time it took for the new King to be crowned, and it was maintained through years of war and hardship until eventually her philosophical acceptance of her own personal tragedies put her in a class above all others.

In doing so she helped to transform the very nature of the monarchy. Photographs of King George V or Queen Mary really enjoying themselves – there is one of his friendly meeting with a young urchin at Sunderland in 1917, another of his riding with Queen Mary in a miniature train at the Empire Exhibition at Wembley in 1924, and so on – are few and far between, but the Queen Mother seems not only to have taken the remoteness out of royalty without risking its essential dignity nor very much

of its mystery, but to have personally persuaded, possibly merely by example, other members of her family to follow suit. For some it has been easier than for others – hence the criticisms of the 1950s and the big public relations push of the 1960s and 1970s – but for the Queen Mother there has never been any need for a swift change of course or style. Hers has evolved gradually, imperceptibly, as the world around her has changed. A former Principal of London University, Sir Douglas Logan, quoted from Shakespeare's Anthony and Cleopatra to illustrate her continuing relevance to everyday life – "Age cannot wither her, nor custom stale her infinite variety . . ."

Indeed, her Chancellorship of London University, which lasted from 1955 to 1980, gave her the opportunity of showing that even as a great-grandmother she appeals as much to the young as to people of her own age. She attended in twenty five years almost every award ceremony, every thanksgiving service and every Students' Union Ball that her health permitted, and President after President of the Union have testified to her charm, untiring interest and her

It was all smiles on 28th October 1982 when the Queen Mother attended the reception at the Press Club, on the very day of its centenary. As the first honorary lady member of the Club she was of course the prime candidate for *the position of cutter of the centenary cake (above) and she brandished a dangerously broad knife as a playful symbol of possible retributions for pressmen who fall foul of royal displeasure. The Press Club likes to keep things in the* *family of course, and chose the occasion to ask the Queen Mother to unveil a portrait of her grandson the Prince of Wales, who is the Club's patron (opposite page, top right). The portrait, by Henry Mee, now hangs in the Club's dining* *room, next to one of the Duke of Edinburgh. Among those presented was John Gerard, editor of the UK Press Gazette, whose glasses collapsed just as he was being introduced. "What you need," said the Queen Mother, "is a paper clip."*

winning effect on them personally. When she retired in 1980, they presented her with a beautiful scroll, recording their appreciation and good wishes. It ended "Love and kisses." That really tickled her.

Although she has an automatic huge public following, she is not one to court public favour wittingly. In the thirty and more years since her daughter came to the throne, she has never meddled in or tried unduly to influence the way in which Queen Elizabeth II and Prince Philip preside over our national affairs. She is conspicuously absent at the annual opening of Parliament, a token of her realisation that constitutionally she has no place in Britain's national life, except as occasional Counsellor of State during the sovereign's absences abroad. Similarly, she does not attend the welcoming ceremonies for State visitors to this country, restricting her involvement to hosting each one for a brief hour in the privacy of Clarence House on the afternoon of their arrival, and attending the State banquets with all the other invited members of the Royal Family. At the Remembrance Sunday Service and at Trooping the Colour she is a spectator rather than a participant, while her daughter discharges her functions as Head of State. At the same time, she keeps in constant touch with the Queen, as indeed with all her family, personally. There are at least two telephone conversations between them every day, at least when both are in Britain, providing desirable and necessary interludes – particularly for the Queen whose day is usually thick with audiences, investitures, visits, meetings or private paper work. One of the Queen's aides once said of these telephone calls that the most amusing thing about them is that when the Queen

Mother telephones through and asks to be connected, he then telephones the Queen and announces "Your Majesty? Her Majesty, Your Majesty."

For a member of the Royal Family living, as it were, on her own and with a diary of engagements now averaging less than two a week, it seems strange, and to some, wrong that she should benefit from the Civil List to the tune of £321,000 per year, almost double Prince Philip's allowance and almost

Almost every member of the Royal Family makes a point of participating in some way or other in the festivals and ceremonies connected with Remembrance Sunday in mid-November each year. In 1982, the Queen Mother maintained her long-standing association with all three of London's major official events. For her in particular, some of whose brothers, nephews and cousins were killed, wounded or taken prisoner in two World Wars, these traditional national commemorations are more than mere ceremonial. Remembrance Sunday itself witnesses the most solemn manifestation – the Service of Remembrance which embraces the laying of wreaths by several members of her family at the Cenotaph in Whitehall. The Queen Mother's own wreath has, since the death of King George VI been placed for her, while she looks down from the balcony of the old Home Office – here she is seen with King Olav of Norway, the Princess of Wales and Princess Alice in 1981

three times those of Princess Anne or Princess Margaret. The answer lies in the Queen Mother's unique rank as widow of a sovereign, which entitles her to a home, a staff and a way of life close to what she would have enjoyed as the King's consort. Consequently, she has a staff of over three dozen – some of whom are on duty part time, and many of whom are unpaid. The unsalaried members of her household are usually old friends holding honorary appointments after many years of faithful service, and her ladies-in-waiting (called Women of the Bedchamber if they attend her on day to day occasions, and Ladies of the Bedchamber if on ceremonial

(left) and again in 1982 (above), and additionally with Princess Anne, Captain Mark Phillips and Princess Michael of Kent (top right) in 1980. There is a more relaxed atmosphere at the annual Festival of Remembrance – a colourful spectacular organised by the Royal British Legion – at the Royal Albert Hall on the eve of Remembrance Sunday (top left), and even at the gathering, usually a couple of days before, at which the Queen Mother always plants a wooden cross in the Royal British Legion's Field of Remembrance at St Margaret's Westminster (opposite page and overleaf). Her Majesty has performed this ceremony for many years during her daughter's reign of almost a third of a century.

duties) go on and off duty in rota, each "shift" lasting from four to six weeks. Between them they keep Clarence House running efficiently both as an administrative enterprise geared to the necessities of the Queen Mother's official life, and as a home, offering her the comforts to which she has become accustomed.

For all that efficiency, she has for many years been indulgently believed to be notoriously unpunctual. This is normally an

her every excuse for making short work of her official duties, is a measure of the importance she attaches to continuing that work while she has the power to do so. Her few illnesses, especially in recent years, have been trivial indeed – the occasional chill and bout of 'flu, the leg ulcer which almost kept her away from the Prince of Wales' wedding in 1981, but which just healed in time, the brief cold which prevented her from joining the rest of her family for the customary Christmas Day Morning Service at St George's Chapel Windsor Castle – all bear satisfactory comparison with those lengthy

indispositions which interrupted her honeymoon in 1923, kept her out of action at the time of the death of King George V and again at the Accession of King George VI, or postponed a tour or two in the mid 1960s. Her little brush with the fishbone in November 1982 accentuated her eagerness not to let small matters get in the way of what she clearly enjoys – a job of work which, in its own way and following her own lights, adds to the quality of an all too mundane life today. The "touch of the twinkle which she keeps for old friends" is now a regular accompaniment to even the most ordinary of duties. It is a

unforgiveable weakness in any member of the Royal Family, whose schedules are worked out months in advance and usually timed to the minute. Queen Victoria and Queen Mary were both models of punctuality – the latter was even born on the very day she was expected – but the Queen Mother, like Queen Alexandra who was, it is said, late for her own Coronation, tends to let the minutes slip by. What Cecil Beeton had praised as her movements "in slow motion" can evidently have disadvantages. There is a belief that she has a notice on her

desk saying in large capital letters DO IT NOW, and an equally widespread counter belief that she has never thought it to have had the slightest effect on her. In effect, any lack of punctuality is more often than not of the type which can always be embraced with cheerfulness, namely that which springs from a consuming interest in whom she is meeting, and what she is doing. It is rarely her arrivals that are late – it is the getting away again.

That this tolerable weakness still exists today, when her advanced years if nothing else would give

trait by which her family have been greatly influenced over the years and which has undoubtedly helped to modernise the monarchy while keeping her young both in spirit and in the esteem of her daughter's subjects. That, in a cynical age when true esteem is hard to come by, is no mean achievement and is ample reward for the long life of dedication, wisdom and inspiration which Queen Elizabeth the Queen Mother has put at the service of her country and of the family whose duty it is in perpetuity to reign over it.

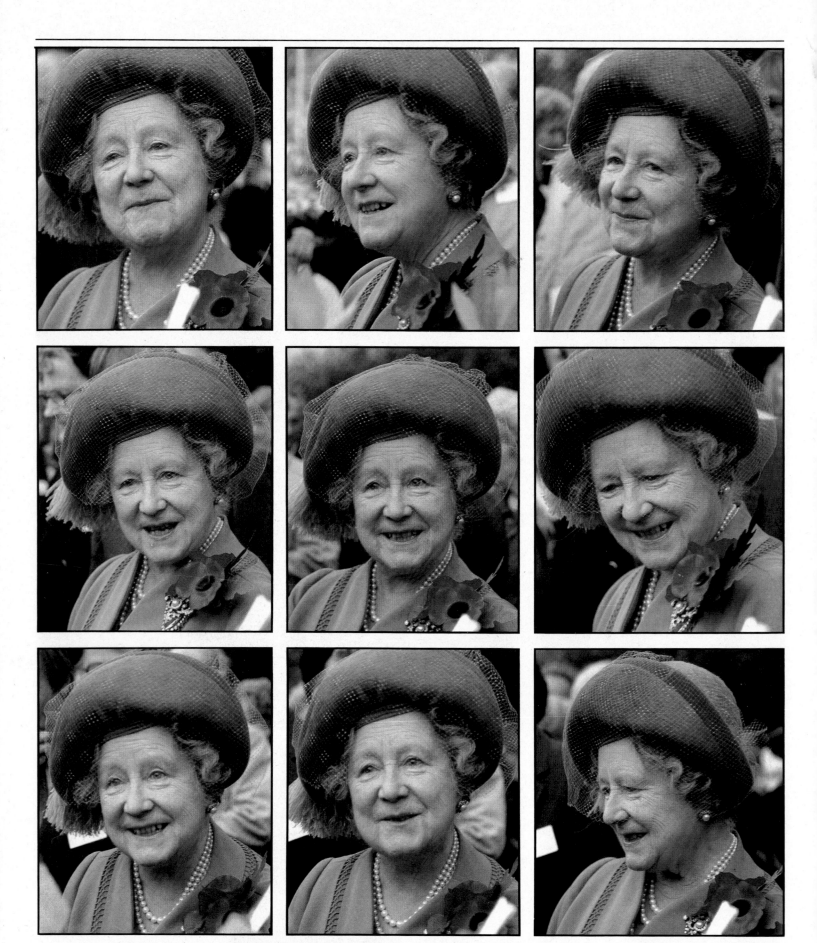

At 82, the Queen Mother still puts everything into her public appearances. At Hyde Park in November 1982, inaugurating the Beautiful Britain campaign she was as animated as ever, revelling in her evident popularity, rewarding it with the concern, kindness and sheer fun which have for sixty years marked her out as the most lovable member of the Royal Family.

FEATURING THE PHOTOGRAPHY OF DAVID LEVENSON - KEYSTONE PRESS AGENCY, LONDON.
First English edition published by Colour Library International Ltd.
© 1983 Illustrations and Text: Colour Library International Ltd.
   99 Park Avenue, New York, N.Y. 10016, U.S.A.
This edition published by British Heritage Press, distributed by Crown Publishers, Inc.
h g f e d c b a
Colour separations by REPROCOLOR LLOVET, Barcelona, Spain.
Display and text filmsetting by ACESETTERS LTD., Richmond, Surrey, England.
Printed and bound in Barcelona, Spain by JISA-RIEUSSET and EUROBINDER.
All rights reserved.
Library of congress catalog card number: 83-71330.
BRITISH HERITAGE PRESS 1983.